AROUND ITALY

Around Italy

2011–2019

VIRGINIA SALINSKY LANDGREEN

LUMINARE PRESS

WWW.LUMINAREPRESS.COM

Around Italy: 2011–2019
Copyright © 2020 by Virginia Salinsky Landgreen

Printed in the United States of America

Cover Design by Kristen Brack

Luminare Press
442 Charnelton St.
Eugene, OR 97401
www.luminarepress.com

LCCN: 2020920889
ISBN: 978-1-64388-499-8

For Sarah and Ian

Vipiteno
Merano
Bolzano
Dobbiaco
Bressanone
Silandro
Adige
Cortina d'Ampezzo
Livigno
Chiavenna
Ora
Tolmezzo
Tarvisio
Colico
Sondrio
Edolo
TRENTINO-ALTO ADIGE
Pieve di Cadore
Domodossola
Bormio
Malè
Belluno
Verbania
Bellagio
Lovere
Riva del Garda
Trento
Feltre
Pordenone
Udine
Aosta
Courmayeur
Lecco
Rovereto
Conegliano
Gorizia
Varese
Como
Lago di Como
Lago di Garda
Monfalcone
Biella
Bergamo
Portogruaro
Grado
Ceresole Reale
Brescia
Bassano del Grappa
Groscavallo
Milano (Milan)
Vicenza
Treviso
Eraclea
Trieste
Susa
Cirié
Novara
Lodi
Verona
Padova
Venezia (Venice)
Sestriere
Vercelli
Pavia
Adige
Lido di Venezia
Turino (Turin)
Asti
Alessandria
Mantova
Nogara
Monselice
Chioggia
Accegio
Busca
Bra
Alba
Piacenza
Cremona
Po
Rovigo
Cuneo
Ceva
Salsomaggiore
Parma
Modena
Ferrara
Mondovì
Genova (Genoa)
Reggio nell'Emilia
Comacchio
Limone Piemonte
Voltri
Savona
Sestri Levante
Bologna
Ravenna
Ventimiglia
Finale Ligure
Aulla
Cervia
Imperia
La Spezia
Carrara
Forlì
Rimini
San Remo
Massa
Cesena
Bordighera
Forte dei Marmi
Pistoia
Bagno di Romagna
Lucca
Prato
Pesaro
Viareggio
SAN MARINO
Fano
Pisa
Livorno
Pontassieve
Urbino
I.di Gorgona
Arno
Firenze (Florence)
Senigallia
Cecina
Arezzo
Città di Castello
Jesi
Ancona
Voltera
Siena
Tevere
I.di Capraia
Montepulciano
Cortona
Gubbio
Macerata
Piombino
Roccastrada
Perugia
Potenza
Civitanova Marche
Chianciano Terme
Fermo
Porto San Giorgio
Follonica
Grosseto
Ombrone
Arcidosso
Todi
Ascoli Piceno
San Benedetto del Tronto
I. Pianosa
Isola d'Elba
Bolsena
Spoleto
Teramo
I.di Montecristo
I. di Giglio
Montefiascone
Terni
Roseto degli Abruzzi
Montalto di Castro
Viterbo
Antrodoco
Atri
Silvi Marina
I. di Giannutri
Tarquinia
Rieti
Penne
Pescara
L'Aquila
Ortona
Chieti

Troia
Puggia
Barletta Trani
Bari
Formia
Terracina
Gaeta
Benevento
Ariano Irpino
Cerignola
Canosa
Andria
Monopoli
Napoli (Naples)
Caserta
Calitri
Lavello
Bitonto
Fasano
Isole Ponziane
I. Ventotene
Pozzuoli
Avellino
Melfi
Altamura
Gioia del Colle
Martina Franca
Brindisi
Torre del Greco
Potenza
Matera
Manduria
I. d'Ischia
Sorrento
Salerno
Corleto Perticara
Ferrandina
Taranto
Lecce
I. di Capri
Agropoli
Roccadaspide
Sala Consilina
Scanzano Jonico
Otranto
Vallo della Lucania
Montesano sulla Marcellana
Maglie
Sapri
Camerota
Lauria
Senise
Gallipoli
Maratea
Gagliano del Capo
Castrovillari
Sibari
Spezzano Albanese
Belvedere Marittimo
Rossano
Cariati
Acri
San Giovanni in Fiore
Paola
Cirò Marina
Cosenza
Crotone
Nicastro
Sersale
Isola Stromboli
Isola di Ustica
Isole Eolie
(Aeolian Islands)
Pizzo
Vibo Valentia
Catanzaro
Soverato
Gioia Tauro
Isola Lipari
Messina
Taurianova
Palermo
Sant'Agata di Militello
Milazzo
Locri
Isole Egadi
Trapani
Erice
Cefalù
Villa San Giovanni
Reggio di Calabria
Barcellona
Pozzo di Gotto
Marsala
Alcamo
Termini Imerese
Mistretta
Randazzo
Castelvetrano
Corleone
Nicosia
Adrano
Mazara del Vallo
Lercara Friddi
Acireale
Sciacca
Aragona
Enna
Caltanissetta
Catania
Agrigento
Canicatti
Lentini
Palma di Montechiaro
Ravanusa
Caltagirone
Augusta
Licata
Gela
Ragusa
Syracuse
Sicilia (Sicily)
Modica
Noto
Ispica

Contents

Prologue

Bridget and Bruno became a couple rather late in life. Both had moved to Eugene, Oregon, as young adults in the mid 1970s but didn't meet until decades later, when they were in their forties. Bridget held fast to "the best is yet to come" while she bided her time, never giving up hope of finding a partner who cared for her. Then she met Bruno.

When they met she was dark-haired, with olive skin tone and dark eyes. He had light brown hair, blue eyes, and skin that didn't tan. Now their hair had changed to white. Bridget had a dancer's body when they became an item, but not for long: Bruno's cooking got to her heart and her waist. While they grew old together, they kept a youthful outlook.

For both of them, making a living in Eugene required entrepreneurship. The northwest's thriving timber industry declined in the 1970s, and the 1980s brought a major recession.

Each developed successful careers. Bruno created prominent art projects in glass for the Eugene Public Library, the University of Oregon, the Eugene Police Headquarters, Lane Transit District's Eugene Station, and the Hult Center for the Performing Arts in addition to numerous residential commissions. Since 2012, his bread and butter has been the repair and restoration of windows and old lamps, work that he continues to do daily at his studio near the railroad tracks.

Bridget retired after thirty years of educating children. She taught swimming and dance, worked in Early Childhood Education at the YMCA and the University of Oregon, and for sixteen years owned and directed a private preschool—West Town Day School.

When they met, Sarina, Bridget's daughter, was living in Portland and her son Jaan was moving from Eugene to Charlottesville, Virginia, where he had spent part of his youth. He had recently graduated from the University of Oregon. Bruno's stepdaughter Rosaria lived with the couple off and on for two years before traveling and relocating.

When the couple became empty nesters, Bridget sold her house and bought a condo on the twelfth floor of a downtown high-rise. Their footprint shrank considerably. With a conscious effort she managed their budget, enabling them to travel to Italy for a month, and sometimes two, every couple of years. They developed a long-term love affair with the country and were nurtured by the beauty they found traveling around Italy and Croatia. Their shared memories bound them closer together, and they could not resist planning "one more" trip. "Kicking around the boot," they called it, but their trips were not made on a big expense account. They worked and saved for their overseas adventures, passing on many activities and traveling smart once they got there.

Bridget loved observing the Italian culture and enjoying the food and wine. A country that put the face of Maria Montessori on their equivalent of the $1 bill (before Italy changed to euros) reflected Bridget's belief in the value of early childhood education.

Bruno devoured Italian history, art, and architecture,

and he was a serious student of the language. He began a local Italian conversation group and read Italian newspapers and books to keep his language skills fresh between trips. His early Catholic school years gave him background for identifying the stories in all of the sacred art they enjoyed.

It suited them to live simply. Socializing with friends, planning trips, living the Italian life while touring, and remembering their sweet times when they returned home fulfilled them. They also enjoyed spending time with their busy family.

During their May 2001 trip, Bridget's children, Sarina and Jaan, plus Bruno's stepdaughter, Rosaria, stayed with them for part of the time in their rented apartment in Florence. Just as Bridget and Bruno had hoped, the experience brought the family closer. Jaan joined them again in Italy 2003 and 2008 and Rosaria also met them for three nights in 2013. In addition they had many people they were close to join them during their stays in Florence and Assisi over the years.

This is the story of the five trips they made between 2011 and 2019. It is a fiction, full of facts and whimsy, and written as a partial record and a full-bodied pleasure.

Rome

In the spring of 2011, Bridget and Bruno spent four nights in Rome, eleven in Assisi, and eight in Ortygia, the historical center of the Sicilian city Siracasa. When they arrived in Rome in the middle of April, they really had an appetite for Italy. They hadn't been since 2008, and wondered then if they would ever be able to return. The financial world had careened to the cliff's edge while they were in Florence two and a half years earlier, but this visit held nothing of that dark cloud. In fact, it was the opposite: Lady Luck was on their side the entire trip.

They left Hotel Mariano, near Rome's central train station Termini, after a catch-up nap in their room and ventured out for their first Italian delight. They passed up the first bar (Bar Eugenio) waiting to find that more perfect bar/café with umbrellas but one that was not too fancy. When they sat and ordered their first house Italian wine the waiter brought them a bottle of Da Vinci Chianti. They could buy this wine at Safeway in their home town Eugene for $10 for a whole bottle, but here they paid $20 (14 euros) for three-quarters of one.

They laughed at how their Italian travel edge had worn dull. At least they were in Rome and there is something very special about that first glass of wine in Italy. Feeling a bit foolish, they found a corner store to pick up some food and wine to take back to the room for later as they watched Italian TV: the news, movies, and specials. They loved it all.

In the morning, after a fairly standard tourist breakfast at the hotel (cream cornetto or a plain roll, cereal, coffee from a machine, yogurt, juice), all closely supervised by a matron in uniform with an evil eye so that none would be taken back to the room, they started their first adventure. They had been prepped by their friends, Angela and Jerry Ross, to visit the Trastevere (across the Tiber) neighborhoods where Angela and Jerry had spent a month the previous fall at the American Academy. Jerry had a painting studio there. Angela had first traveled to Italy using an organization where guests could stay for one night in homes of members in order to promote peace and international understanding. She and Jerry had returned many times to Italy. They were excellent ambassadors. Angela studied Italian in Perugia for one year, which made exchanges easy for the handsome couple.

Bruno and Bridget took the #75 bus to the top of the hill and discovered a perfect point to view the city. It was Rome's equivalent of the famous Florence viewpoint Piazzale Michelangelo.

There were several monuments, including one to Garibaldi and one to his wife Anita. Angela had told them about the monument to Anita who fought by Garibaldi's side during the unification of Italy in 1849. In the large memorial she is depicted on a raging horse, hair flying in the wind, with a gun in one hand and a nursing baby in the other. A few months after the unification campaign, she died. The stories of their passion for each other touched Bridget deeply. The walk down into old Rome also had a *passeggio* (formal

Italian walkway) lined with busts of war heroes. Bruno and Bridget encountered school children on field trips in this park, with their teachers dedicated to herding them through while exposing them to culture.

Bruno and Bridget made up for the previous night's small dinner by returning to a trattoria near the Pantheon by 1:00 in the afternoon. On a previous trip they had a great time in its adjoining wine store. This was Bridget's kind of place. No signage of any kind, but inside locals were ordering what was good for the day (and it was good). Eating was one of their main events in Italy and they tried to dine before 2 p.m. as the Italians do. Bruno and Bridget shared roasted eggplant, cooked greens, bread, pasta with a cream and pancetta sauce, and wine.

There is no need to buy bottled water in Rome. Roman water is excellent from the tap. It is called *acqua del rubinetto*, *acqua del sindaco*, or *acqua della mano*. Many fountains have a spigot where you can fill your water bottle with cold mountain water. It tastes as good as Willamette Valley water. Suddenly, jet lag hit Bridget like a lead balloon (one of her mother's expressions). They headed back to their very comfortable hotel where Bridget could rest while Bruno ventured out.

Later they visited some nearby basilicas and churches. In the evening they strolled around and found a *tavola calda* (hot table) where, for 7 euros, they had a spread of tapas-like Italian delights and a really good cocktail, a Negroni (equal parts sweet vermouth, Campari, and gin with a lemon peel). They went back to this find two more times during their four days in Rome.

On their final two days, they opted for the double-decker tourist bus. From the bus seats they circled and saw the main monuments five or six times, plus they could hop off at areas they wanted to explore.

Bruno had done a spectacular job of navigating bus and train schedules. Their visit spanned Easter, May 1st, the beatification of Pope Giovanni Paolo II, the royal wedding, Mother's Day, and the April 25th commemoration of the day the Allies landed during WWII. They would be in Assisi for most of these events. Every holiday created exceptions to the bus and train schedules. They learned the word *dipende* (it depends) as it applied to the holiday variations of schedules.

Travelers could spend a month in Rome and not begin to scratch the surface. Staying near the train station, Bridget and Bruno peeked into many bauble shops. These were street-level or basement-level stores that featured costume jewelry, scarves, dresses, and beads that the refugee population hawks from blankets and in the markets. They ended up purchasing a few gifts in these item-packed holes-in-the-walls , although probably all of the goods were made in China.

Villa d'Este

As always, Bridget enjoyed the train trip. They were headed to Tivoli, nineteen miles from Rome, for a three-day visit. They went to see the villa and gardens of Villa d'Este, a masterpiece and UNESCO world heritage site. The hotel for their two nights in Tivoli was close to the train station. Often this means that the section of town is run down, and it was true here. The hotel's description of being 100 yards from the station didn't mention that guests had to cross a bridge over a river and carry their luggage up a few hundred steps to get to the hotel from the train. Their room was simple. The staff person who checked them in was cheerful and helpful. It only took them a little while to settle in.

As they explored the neighborhood they discovered Flo's, a fancy bar with a wall of windows that looked out over the town. They had an aperitivo as the sun was setting. They also returned the next night for an aperitivo and enough complimentary snacks to practically ruin their appetites.

That evening, after dining on some take-out food and a bottle of wine, they settled in their room to relax with Italian television. They wanted to be rested up for a big day with an early start.

Waking to a cool, sunny morning, the two travelers stopped at a bar for a cappuccino and fresh cornetto.

An Italian bar serves many a *caffè* (espresso) throughout the day. Pastries and cappuccinos are common in the morning, and *panini* (small sandwiches) are made up ahead and in the case. A few tiny tables may be available, but the coffees are usually consumed in a few sips by standing patrons. Selected liquors are on display and available, but the caffè drinkers throughout the day provide most of the business.

On they walked to the Villa and its extraordinary gardens full of fountains, statues of nymphs, grottoes, plays of water, and baroque styles. It was even more spectacular than they could have imagined.

There were several large groups of middle-school students frolicking in and around the hedges and fountains. The whimsy captured in Baroque and Mannerist styles brought out playfulness in everyone. Oh, what fun those Italians escaping the heat must have had! Inside the palace were large oil paintings of people bathing *au naturel* in the large pools with a background like the hanging gardens of Babylon. The Renaissance genius for tunneling an aqueduct underground joined with the vision of painter-architect-archeologist Pirro Ligorio and realized by court architect Alberto Galvani was as grand as it gets.

The garden inspired a lot of photos. Bruno looked especially handsome with his short-cropped hair, necktie, and tailored jacket. After a full week, the vacation had taken hold and they were both relaxed and in their element. Bridget squeezed Bruno's hand and stole a few kisses as the morning progressed.

How would she have known about this place without her mate? In truth, Bridget could barely find her way at all in Italy. Her sense of direction was nearly 100% wrong which left her feeling vulnerable and dependent on Bruno when they traveled. Her Italian would not be much help, either, if she ever did get lost. It had never happened, but she was sure that she would be in a panic if it ever did. Unlike her usual independence at home, she clung to Bruno.

All of the fanciful touches that her eyes beheld tickled Bridget. There was an air of lightness in humor and style that was so pleasing about the garden.

After a few hours of walking they left the villa. They stopped and stood at a bar for panini and a glass of wine before they headed back to the hotel. Bruno later went by bus to nearby Villa Adriana—Hadrian's Villa, and Bridget got into her wool socks and silk kimono and napped. That evening they would eat out.

Their hotel owner had been very kind to them. She brought them pastries and coffee and cookies during their stay and recommended a family run *osteria* (a simple restaurant) for their last meal in Tivoli.

As usual they were the first to arrive at 7, early by Italian dining standards, and still had to wait half an hour for the service to start. Soon families with young children drifted in. Most of the tables filled up and the crowd enjoyed great food and the gaiety Italians bring to eating together.

Bruno and Bridget split a large salad and pasta dish. This place felt like the hub of the working town. Thinking about the garden they had seen, Bridget wondered if everyone in the town's center, the *centro città*, worked at the villa when it was inhabited by Cardinal Ippolito II d'Este, who lived there after his failed bid for the papacy in the late 1500's. It could have taken many people living in the ancient town to assist with what must have been very grand goings-on.

Bruno and Bridget held hands as they found their way home in the dark. They began to pack for the next day's trip by train into Umbria and Assisi, where they would stay for almost two weeks in the apartment they had rented on a previous visit.

As they carried their suitcases to the station, Bridget noted how much easier the hundreds of steps were to climb down than up. Their train wound its way through the countryside, and they could see hill towns in the distance. In Assisi there would be family and friends to visit.

Assisi

*T*hey traveled by train and bus to Assisi where their friend Mara lived, having moved from Eugene five years previously. Bridget and Bruno rented an apartment adjoining hers in the upper level of the city (Sopra), near San Rufino Cathedral. They were there for 11 nights, and for five of them their friends, George Filgate and Patricia Marshall, rented the second bedroom in their spacious apartment. It had a kitchen, a large enough dining area, and a TV.

Mara greeted Bridget and Bruno with homemade gnocchi and a salad of greens and blood oranges. She also mixed prosecco with the blood orange juice. They had landed well.

The next two days were spent going to buy provisions for Easter dinner, never mind art and sightseeing. One trip by train took them to a favorite cheese and salami shop in the next town. Anyone who knows Mara knows that she is all about food and cats.

In fact, she has the distinction of being one of a dozen gattare in Assisi. This is a band of mostly women who get up at five each morning and make the rounds, feeding the cats around the hill town. She is shown appreciation by being given all of the wine and olive oil that she can use.

Mara is a great shopper, and she often arrives just as the green grocer is about to throw out a laundry basket of field greens. Mara takes them off his hands and cooks them slowly for a long time. They ate the equivalent of a pasture one night! Even the nettles and thistles cooked down nicely. Mara loves cheese and salami and knows where every good bite is to be found.

Bridget met Mara in 1980 when Bridget was slender and had no interest in cooking. Mara, on the other hand, had worked at the Metropol bakery and was the main pastry chef at Café Zenon in Eugene. Mara later became a marriage and family counselor. She was in her late sixties and Bridget thought she looked like Helen Mirren. She was quick and even more nimble since moving to Italy and living in a hill town.

On the evening of Maundy Thursday they went into San Rufino as parishioners took down the wooden Christ (with hinged arms changed from outstretched to by his side) from the cross and placed him on a narrow bed with red satin dust ruffle, blanket, and pillow. Maundy Thursday commemorates the Last Supper of Jesus Christ with the Apostles. Christ took and shared bread and wine, just as Christians continue to celebrate the Eucharist today. The church was so crowded that it seemed that the whole parish had arrived after work. Everyone gathered around the Christ statue lying in the bed. Young and old lovingly touched him. An elderly woman tenderly straightened his crown of thorns and kissed his robe. A seven year old boy, mesmerized, hovered near, touching Christ even longer than the rest.

The following night, when it was dark, all of the clergy in town, in their long processional robes, carried Christ in this bed from the top of the hill at San Rufino down to the basilica of San Francesco (Saint Francis) at the bottom of the vertical town, passing by several old churches on the way. They were led by a single drummer who sounded a mournful heartbeat on his drum. The clergy had torches to light the way. A statue of Mary as Our Lady of Sorrows, with seven swords piercing her chest, was transported along the route. Nothing like this had ever happened in the Lutheran church where Bridget grew up in Ohio. She loved the pageantry and it touched her spiritual nature in a way the more reserved religious practices had failed to do.

Assisi is known as the home of the patron saint of Italy, St. Francis. Immediately following the Easter service the town transforms itself into competition mode for their Calendimaggio extravaganza. The three day festival loosely ties in with the May Day celebration. Assisi is turned into its medieval alter ego, and the upper and lower levels of the town compete in many areas: drumming, costumes, singing, and food.

Their friends George and Patricia arrived the day before Easter. Because of the holiday bus schedule, they had to drag heavy suitcases uphill for over an hour (in some of the only rain Bridget and Bruno encountered during their trip) to get to the apartment. Finally, they achieved a joyous reunion, fueled by the local wine and an onion pizza from the shop down the street. Bridget thought traveling with friends brought the good times back home.

None of them made the Easter service at San Rufino the next day. Bruno cooked his perfect poached eggs and around noon Patricia and Bridget wandered to the church just as bread, salami, and sweet red wine were served to the parishioners. They joined the group.

There were plans to go to Mara's friend, Laurie's, so they were saving room for the Easter feast of cheese, salami, and olive antipasti, then asparagus risotto, roast lamb, three kinds of potatoes, blood orange and greens salad, and wines. They would also have a dessert made by Mara and coffee at their hostess Laurie's condo, which was in an old castle. There were nine of them around the table, including Laurie's two teenaged boys.

They decided to check out the roof terrace as a site for dessert. Five of the diners loaded into the elevator, joking about the weight limit. Luckily their new friend Rosa had decided to walk up the stairs with her dog and cell phone. The group of five ended up getting stuck between floors in the elevator for over an hour. Nobody had a cell phone and there wasn't a phone in the elevator.

Bridget began the joke-telling. Rather than panic about finding a repair person on Easter in Italy, they took pictures with someone's camera and moved on to singing songs. Everything turned out OK when the go-to guy (every condo has one) was found a half hour away. He came from his Easter dinner to climb into the elevator shaft to save them.

That was two miracles…something like coming out of a tomb, they thought. The other miracle was that nobody had to go to the bathroom while stuck in the elevator.

Somehow, during the ordeal, the little dog had gotten out of Rosa's sight and had mounted the table and finished their meal. Bridget was exhausted and not a bit hungry anyway.

On the day after Easter, it is the custom to have a picnic with Easter leftovers. Since rain threatened, Bridget and Bruno invited the Easter lunch group and a few more friends of Mara's to their apartment for lunch. Bridget felt very full from all the eating.

The days were peppered with visits to nearby shops, churches, and art installations. They did take Mara to her favorite trattoria, La Rocca, near the fortress that overlooked the upper town. The food was excellent and reasonable and they shared dishes so that they could try many.

One day Bridget, Bruno, Patricia, and George traveled into Perugia by bus. They went to the Umbrian regional art museum in the old civic building. Even short trips take time. They waited for buses maybe three hours that day. It helped to be passing the time with old friends. All three of George and Patricia's daughters, Ellen, Claire, and Christine, had gone to West Town Day School. This was the small school that Bridget had owned and directed. For many years she saw this family on a daily basis. Bruno knew Patricia back in Maryland, when she was twelve and he was nineteen. Patricia and George were a very talented couple and easy to be with. George was an IT manager, photographer, and drummer, Patricia an editor, writer, and entrepreneur.

The next day George and Patricia traveled on to Venice and Bruno and Bridget prepared to watch the royal wedding of Prince William and Kate Middleton on TV. Mara, Bruno, their new friend Suzanne and Bridget watched this event while having lunch in their apartment. Bridget had brought a large black straw hat for the televised wedding. Having been to a beautiful wedding in England, she knew that wearing a hat can be an important element for a woman at a British wedding. Bruno was impressed with her black hat.

After dark that evening Mara scampered Bruno and Bridget up and around the hills to a performance by the festival choir. Time stood still for Bridget as twenty trained voices sang medieval love songs in a tiny piazza. She looked up to the four-story building in the background. On one balcony a mother, daughter and grandmother stood and listened. Above them an older couple huddled close to each other for this memorable serenade. Bridget felt it was one of the sweetest moments ever.

Events were happening left and right leading up to the beginning of Calendimaggio. Men in black tights practiced the flag toss pageantry accompanied by thirty costumed drummers ranging in age from five to eighty-five. Bridget agreed with Mara that the men looked great in tights! The *taverna* (temporary trattoria) where they ate opened up to feed the participants and expected crowds.

Before departing for Sicily, Mara took Bruno and Bridget to her favorite country inn for lunch. This was a half hour walk out of town or a short distance by car. The food was cooked over a blazing fire. All of the meat as well as the other roasted vegetables were crisped to perfection.

On their next to last day, Bridget and Bruno traveled by train to Spello in the region of Umbria. Spello is referred to as Assisi's little sister. It is smaller and every bit as beautiful. They visited several churches and a very small municipal art gallery in an old palazzo.

Spello is known for the Infiorata Festival (the city streets feature designs made of flower petals) which would happen in a few months. Bridget felt like a tourist again, walking the cobblestones with Bruno and holding his hand as they crossed the streets.

On the way home they stopped in a tiny town at a *macelleria* (butcher shop) for some salami, at Mara's request. Their thoughts were straying ahead to cleaning the apartment and preparing for their big travel day when they would leave Mara (sigh) and Assisi at 6 a.m. and go by bus, train, train, plane, bus, and final bus to Ortygia in Sicily where they would spend the second half of their trip.

Sicily

Bridget and Bruno were headed to the southeastern Sicilian coast. Rome was the furthest south Bridget had been; for Bruno, it was his second trip to Sicily. Their small plane landed at Sicily's Catania airport. The island of Sicily is the round ball that the boot of Italy is kicking. Once outside the terminal, they stood waiting for the bus to take them to Siracusa.

They waited so long that they began to feel uneasy about being in the right place. The bus stop was scrappy-looking, with no redeeming qualities. The group of Italians waiting with them were burdened with luggage. A young, street-weary man offered to give them a cab ride. They watched him as he bent over to get money out of one sock and some other important papers from the other sock. He told them his service would cost 60 euros (at that time $100). They said they were not interested.

Finally the bus arrived and they settled in for the ride. Bruno said he could feel Bridget's spirits sinking as she took in the landscape. Bridget had been apprehensive about traveling in southern Italy. Still, she was not prepared even though she had been girding herself for disappointment. Buildings were abandoned or falling apart. Nothing matched the high style or well-preserved simplicity that she admired about Italy. She found some relief when they went through nine long tunnels that were well lit and had safety signage throughout. After passing no sights to treasure, their bus arrived at the depot in Siracusa where they were to wait for their final bus (the free jitney) that would cross the bridge onto the island of Ortygia.

In Ortygia the sky had greyed and it was sprinkling. They consulted the written directions for their reservation and realized that they had gone past their bus stop. After walking several blocks they arrived at their apartment, only five minutes late to meet Massimo, their rental agent. He checked them into the narrow apartment that would serve as their base for the next eight nights. It had recently been renovated and was modern, crisp, and spacious. A family with two children could easily have been comfortable there. Massimo spoke English, and Bridget's impression of the second Sicilian business person they met was a big improvement over the first, who kept his valuables in his socks.

As Massimo was showing them how to operate their satellite TV, it flashed onto a BBC news report of the death of Osama bin Laden. Bridget could not believe that this man was dead. He had posed a threat for so long. Massimo agreed.

They enjoyed having access to the news in those first few days since, to avoid the extra expense and encumbrance, they were traveling without phone or computer. As well as seeing more news of bin Laden's death, they watched the Italian soap opera *Tempesta d'Amore* as they had during other trips. *Walker, Texas Ranger* and *The Simpsons* were also showing, dubbed in Italian.

The apartment had a large bedroom, a full kitchen, a dining area and a living room. From the small balcony they could see the Mediterranean at the far end of the alley. On the roof there was a lovely private terrace with outdoor furniture. Standing on their tiptoes, they could see the water. At the other end of the alley was a small grocery store. Every day but Sunday Ortygia had a fish market which included vegetables, tons of oranges, plus other fruits, cheeses, meats, pistachios, breads, and baubles. Bruno and Bridget shopped every day and cooked in most nights, savoring the mussels, *gamberetti* (large shrimp), and early spring vegetables.

However, on that first night they dined out. Bruno choose their *trattoria* (slightly less formal than an osteria) well. The tourist season hadn't started so they were seated with only one other couple in a restaurant that several tour books had pointed out for its local dishes. The mixed seafood grill that they shared helped them identify some of the local fish from the varieties they would later see in the market. They ordered a pasta they had never heard of *casarecce* (a short pasta folded in on itself), and later found it in the grocery store. The travelers drank house wine and later found grappa in the store. Grappa is like brandy. It is distilled from the final pressing of grapes including skins and twigs. In Italy it is powerful and reasonably priced (about $12 a bottle instead of $50 in the states). That night Bridget had grappa dreams that went especially deep into her subconscious. They were colorful and full of symbolism that she could hardly remember when she woke. This often happened to her after drinking the strong digestivo.

They woke up and began to explore the island, which proved to be a sweet, beautiful, ancient morsel of Italy. The Greeks and Romans first came to Sicily by way of Ortygia. There were ruins of a Temple to Minerva near the town's outdoor market. It took Bridget and Bruno just over an hour to walk the circumference of the island along a beautiful seawall with a wrought iron railing. The old hotels and homes facing the sea were noble looking and stoutly intact. The population of the town of roughly 125,000 welcomed tourists, unlike the locals at some of Italy's more popular cities.

They especially enjoyed the Jewish section of the town where they found an organic food store, the Mikvah baths, and a *Pupi* (puppet) Opera. The Pupi Opera totally captivated Bridget. For three generations, the Mauceri family has launched productions in Ortygia. Luckily, Bridget and Bruno were able to attend a production in the pocket theatre with seating for an audience of about two dozen. The windowless room was narrow with simple benches for the audience. The puppet master himself scurried into the theatre to sell them tickets before the performance. The play featured marionettes of Orlando, many soldiers, a princess, and magic spells. Bridget had a hard time understanding the Italian, but the story was simple enough to follow and included many sword fights.

Six family members participated in the theatre production. Bridget was inspired by the scope of this creative endeavor, its presence in the small town, and the power that came from sharing history and Sicilian culture.

After the play they went to the Puppet Museum. It featured ten exhibits behind three feet by five feet windows. The puppet master operated the sound effects and lighting. Near the museum was the workshop of the puppet-making family. Bridget made a note to look into marionettes when she was back in Oregon.

That evening Bridget stood on the small balcony. The beauty and scented air inspired her to sort back through her life as she gazed at the street below. Many sweet memories surfaced, especially of her children Sarina and Jaan when they were young. She left the balcony, quietly closing the doors, and joined Bruno, who was fast asleep in bed.

One sunny day Bridget and Bruno took an hour-long ride on a double-decker boat that traveled the circumference of the island. There was a large group of tourists from Germany who were a bit loud and enjoying each other's company and the blissful waterscape. Where it once guarded the entrance to the port was the magnificent *castello* (castle). The tour guide explained it was being renovated by local architecture students.

During their stay in Sicily, Bruno and Bridget traveled from Ortygia back to Siracusa by bus several times, visiting the archeological museum and the adjoining park-like setting for both Roman and Greek amphitheatres. The park contained marble quarries that had been worked by slaves in ancient times. The Roman stadium was in ruins, but the Greek stadium was intact and getting ready to mount its season of classical plays. Bridget was sad they would be leaving before the plays began. Her theatre training in college had produced some of the same classics.

They saw on a poster that, later in the summer, Andrea Bocelli would perform a benefit concert. Bridget had never seen a more romantic venue. From the top of the amphitheatre one could see the Mediterranean, azure blue and filling the far horizon.

She enjoyed observing the southern Italians. The dialect was different, the speech was faster, and the consonants d and t were often dropped. When kisses were planted on both sides of the cheeks of a loved one, they were loud enough to be heard at a distance! Young and old were dressed neatly and with a sense of style, even though unemployment hovered around 20%. Bruno and Bridget read in The Lonely Planet that visitors were advised not to chat about the mafia to the people of Sicily and "yes," the travel guide said, "everyone is connected." When they first arrived in the town a gentleman in a leisure suit had insisted they register their names at the city hall. Never before had this been asked of them. They never asked or understood the meaning of this. Nevertheless, Bruno and Bridget felt very safe because they looked like tourists.

It has since been edited out of his guide book, but Rick Steves suggested that you could enter a pastry shop and ask them to fresh fill your cannoli on the spot. Bruno and Bridget laughed at the thought of a batch of English speaking tourists arriving with the bright idea of requesting this! Sicily is also the home of gelato in a brioche, which looked to Bridget like gelato in a hamburger roll. She didn't have the nerve to try one. They were followers of Rick Steves' travel suggestions in general.

The two travelers took a bus south into the town of Noto one day and enjoyed walking around and viewing the Baroque architecture. They had one of their top meals at a trattoria they learned of from someone on the bus. Once again, it was handy that Bruno spoke Italian and was fond of practicing with strangers. They followed directions to the unremarkable entrance and were pleased to find the kind and quality of meal that kept them coming back to Italy. They ordered another mixed seafood grill, plus pasta with sardines, pine nuts, and raisins. It was all very good and, since they split dishes, not expensive. They laughed to recall that when they began traveling in Italy, in 2001, they thought they had to order from every course and not share plates. Fortunately, they soon learned that was untrue.

     VIRGINIA SALINSKY LANDGREEN

Every time they returned to Ortygia from one of their excursions, Bridget noticed more beauty and peacefulness in the small fishing town. There was not much activity on the water. They saw only two large boats (yachts) and numerous private little fishing boats docked in the small marina. The only bridge from the island to Siracusa was primarily a pedestrian bridge, with room for cars but not buses or trucks. The water that surrounded the island was calm the whole time they were there. The sun was welcome, and the humidity low. They imagined the heat during the dry summer.

Bridget loved being by the water. This trip was especially enjoyable to her, maybe because she had grown up in a house on a lake. As a child she spent long periods of time looking out onto the reflection of light on the water. It still felt peaceful.

On a day trip north to Catania they visited a famous fish market. On tables arranged outside the market, many other things were being offered for sale. In all the fish markets, the vendors did a lot of yelling about their product. Catania had a large historic center and several monuments. When they visited the Duomo, they got swept up into a small wedding crowd that was leaving. Bruno took photos of the bride and groom and Bridget noted similarity between the features of the beautiful bride and Bruno's step-daughter, Rosaria, who has ancestors from Palermo, another Sicilian city.

Bridget carried some sadness at leaving the calm shores of the Mediterranean as they traveled back to Rome for their flight home. The weight of the long trip ahead helped her keep tears in check. She knew that when she got home she would miss wandering hand in hand in Italy with Bruno.

Ice

There was much to do before leaving for the 2013 trip. The routine of going to the gym needed to be kept since Bridget would be walking for hours and lugging at least 40 pounds of luggage around northern Italy for two months.

She loved the feel of her running shoes tied together at the laces and slung over her shoulder just as she had long ago carried her ice skates in the Ohio steel town where she grew up. Today she drove across the bridge from the center of Eugene, joining an exercise class for seniors. Sixty years had passed since she was a girl in Ohio, but what's sixty years to the mysterious workings of the mind?

It seemed like only yesterday that after school, in the darkness, lit by streetlights, she would go down the hill in her backyard which bordered on Lake Glacier, often with her older brother Michael. They knew how to bundle up against the cold: two pairs of socks (one wool), two pairs of pants, two sweaters, a coat, scarf, gloves, and hat, all slightly smelling of moth balls. Also necessary was 25 cents for hot chocolate out of the newly installed vending machine in the boat house. The chocolate was watery but good and warm, often drunk in front of a roaring, crackling fire at the edge of the lake. The fire was tended by a Mill Creek Park security employee

     Virginia Salinsky Landgreen

whose job was to clean the snow off the frozen lake and to keep an eye on the spots where the ice was getting soft. They needed to be ready to fish anyone out if the sawhorses that limited the skating area of the large lake were ignored. There were tales of both adults and children falling into the freezing water through the ice. These were true, but did not happen too often. Bridget didn't know anyone personally who had slipped into the water. All ages skated during the day, as well as in the evening with plenty of streetlights around the lake.

Skating was second nature to Bridget. She was the youngest of three children. Anna and Michael were older. From the time she could walk the entire family would spend a winter weekend afternoon on the ice if they could. Initially she wore the double bladed clip-ons and a snowsuit so puffy that any fall would be cushioned. Papa went with them until that one afternoon when his legs shot out from under him and he landed hard on his seat, not escaping the laughter and teasing from mother, marking his retirement from the ice a family legend. Even at a young age Bridget could understand him not wanting to be laughed at by mother.

After Bridget grew up opportunities for ice skating were rare but not non-existent. Just like riding a bike, you always remember the skill. There would be other ponds, but most often she walked to man-made rinks which were always busy in the long Ohio winters.

Most of the fun Bridget had while she was growing up came in the form of outdoor fun. Now living in the Great Northwest, 3,000 miles away and many years later there was still plenty of fun to be had. In fact, the last time she skated was the previous summer when she'd gone with her granddaughter, Gemma, her sister Anna, and Anna's two oldest grandchildren, Simon and Petra. Bridget counted her close relationship with her sister as one very large gift. They gardened together and checked in with each other regularly.

Besides all that she had learned from her sister, they had a wonderful time and loved to share grandchildren stories and outings. Shopping at garage sales and sharing family meals were just a few of the many things they enjoyed together. Except for their height, they did not resemble each other.

Anna's beautiful red hair was a singular event in the family. Bridget's short, now graying brown hair was more the family norm. Both were tall and strong. Anna had kept her girlish figure. Bridget had blossomed into roundness.

Skating at Portland, Oregon's Lloyd Center shopping mall, five-year old granddaughter Gemma had needed total support around the rink. Simon and Petra had been to skate camp the summer before, and Simon instructed Gemma with great authority. Magically, the awkwardness of an eight-year old boy was transformed to that of a coach. Bridget glimpsed the kind young man he would grow to be. She smiled in disbelief as her granddaughter wriggled her hand free to take Simon's hand and edge forward. "Run as fast as you can, then glide!" Simon instructed with an experienced air. Gemma made mincing steps in place and moved forward three inches, soaking in the attention of her older cousin. Her application of his instruction failed to move her far on the ice but she had followed his words closely.

Bridget came out of her reverie of the past summer and swung her running shoes into the car and drove off to do errands after her Silver Sneakers and yoga class ended.

Being gone for two months would be a long time. Getting past the three-week mark was the trick for her. She would miss her family terribly. It would help to be able to keep in touch since she and Bruno would carry laptops on this trip.

Leaving

In 2003, Bridget and Bruno walked from their high-rise condo in downtown Eugene to the Amtrak train station with their luggage in tow. They returned from Europe two months later via the same station, again on foot, a little travel weary, with the clickity-clackity sound of Bridget's rolling suitcase a slight annoyance for the 20 final blocks home.

They had made a stop in Frederick, Maryland at the start and finish to visit Bruno's father Will and his mother Margaret. Will was reaching the end of his life. On their return he was already in the care of hospice and must have had a stroke because he was speaking in a language that only he understood. The sadness of these two visits hung heavy as they traveled home, now knowing that Bruno would be returning to Maryland with hardly any time to unpack. Just two months later Will died with his seven children and beloved wife around him.

In 2003, during their two months in France and Tuscany, Bridget and Bruno had both become adept and blasé about their travels, so much so that, when packing in the hotel, they looked at their return flight from Italy to the U.S. and were horrified to find that they were leaving two hours late. There was still a train trip to the airport in Frankfurt, Germany for their return flight.

Bridget had given up fibbing at the age of 10 after some childhood whoppers. Also, her life as an adult became so complicated that to lie would be a danger. The truth could be remembered; lies were out of the grasp of the memory. Even so, she knew that a small lie at the airport ticket office could mean the difference between a simple reschedule or purchasing two new one-way tickets home, so she boldly stated that the train had been late. When Bruno started to correct her with the truth she shot him a quick elbow to the ribs and, luckily, the heart of the airline agent was moved to reschedule their flight on the next day without cost.

Ten years later they were setting off on another two-month adventure; the excitement was already mounting. They were to fly out of Eugene and arrive in Milan. This time they would check and double-check reservations and departure times. Most of their visit (three weeks) would be spent in an apartment where they had stayed before, adjoining that of their friend Mara, whom they had known for decades.

Mara had become a permanent resident of Assisi 2007. Luigi, once her husband and now a loyal companion, was on an extended visit. He lived separately a few hundred yards away in the upper part of the hill town.

Perhaps Bruno's step-daughter Rosaria would also visit, along with her travelmate Dan.

Bridget and Bruno were also planning to meet Angela and Jerry, who would be traveling from Eugene to the hill towns at the same time. Jerry would, for the second time, have a studio in which to paint at the American Academy in Rome and then he would have several shows of his paintings in different towns in Italy. It always made the memories of travel times richer to connect with family and friends who would remember the adventures and vistas they loved so much. Meals would be recalled, and even mishaps would take on a special humor of their own.

Bridget would miss her beautiful daughter Sarina, and her husband John. They are the doting parents of Gemma. Bridget would also miss her son Jaan (the bachelor) who lives in Charlottesville, Virginia.

Bruno's grasp of the Italian language continued to grow even when at home. His glass studio has many tasks that are repetitive and he can listen to Italian radio. Mastering the dialects, which change from town to town, would take a lifetime. Bridget bumbled along, depending on Bruno to figure out anything complex. Bruno always said that she could "hit it over the net" as a way to describe her level of Italian comprehension and speaking.

Milano

As Bridget and Bruno sat in the waiting area of Newark airport, with conversations carried on in Italian all around them, Bridget realized the trip had begun. Her heartbeat quickened. She reached for Bruno's hand just as he was saying that he wanted to engage in more dialogues with Italians. She then looked across the seating area and the most countrified, presumably southern Italian, man caught her eye. He had dark bushy hair, streaked with grey, tied back in a ponytail under his fedora. He had olive skin that looked like it had seen seasons in the sun. He wore baggy clothes in muted colors. She nudged Bruno and directed his attention to the man. As Bruno looked closer, he was convinced that this was Keith, aka Dmitri, of The Flying Karamazov Brothers, a famous new-age vaudeville troupe. Bruno had seen him perform many times at the Oregon Country Fair.

He went over to greet the man and sure enough it was Keith, who said that he had a 4,000 square foot home in Tuscany. "Somewhere between Bologna and Florence," Keith said, which covers quite a bit of territory. "I suppose he didn't want to encourage us to look him up!" whispered Bridget later.

     VIRGINIA SALINSKY LANDGREEN

After they landed in Milan and arrived at the newly renovated Hotel San Francisco, Bridget and Bruno took a nap and settled in before getting on the subway to explore the center of town. Their destination on that first evening was near the Duomo and the beautiful glass-enclosed Galleria shopping area. They had been in the Rinascente department store in Florence where they enjoyed the top-floor food court, so here in Milan they headed up through a branch of the same store to the top-floor and chose a bistro that featured homemade local cheeses. Bridget had a salad with *valeriana* (a very small-leafed green) and some wonderful hard cheese with honey drizzled over it, served with quince and cherry jelly. There were a few toasted walnuts scattered on the plate. The simplicity and potent flavors reminded her of why they kept coming back to Italy every few years.

They left the store, paying attention to the beautifully displayed merchandise, yet knowing they had neither the room in their suitcases nor the budget for any purchases. Snow was falling on this early March evening as they caught a bus to the hotel and settled in for a night of Italian TV along with some wine, cured meat and crusty bread that they picked up on the way home.

The expression *sogni d'oro* (meaning golden dreams) applied to Bridget's sleep. After a hearty breakfast offered by the hotel (not the typical Italian start of a pastry and a cappuccino), the two set off to explore the city. When they walked through Peck, the most famous food store in Milan, they were not even tempted to make a purchase because they were still so full from breakfast. Next they visited the castello of the Sforzas, once the ruling family of Lombardy. The castle was well preserved and occupied a large piece of land in the center of Milan. It had multiple side buildings and housed a magnificent collection of art. The rooms were large enough to hold the giant pieces of tapestry and sculpture that Bridget and Bruno admired.

The next day they would meet their young friend, Christine, at the fountain in front of the castle. Christine, in her twenties, was spending the year in Milan as an au pair. Visiting Christine was a perfect reason for Bridget and Bruno to have chosen to spend a week in Milan.

After a day of seeing more sights, Bridget watched as Christine approached at the appointed time. Bridget had known her since she was born and had been her caregiver at the childcare center/day school that Bridget had owned and directed. That day in Milan, Christine was dressed in a fitted light green coat with a silk scarf around her neck, woolen stockings, boots, hair pulled back in a loose bun and she wore single pearl earrings. She looked very well put-together, thought Bridget proudly. The three embraced. Bruno had also known Christine her entire life and the sight of her being so independent and happy in one of the most beautiful cities in the world made this sunny crisp day even more memorable.

They walked to the Duomo and took a quick tour and made plans to meet later that evening when Christine and three of her American friends would show them some nightlife.

Bruno and Bridget arrived at 8 p.m. for an aperitivo and buffet of wonderful small bites of Italian cooking called *cicchetti*. The drinks were 9 euros and the snacks were free. It was possible to make a meal of these delights and especially for the young people, who do go out at night, a great way to gather. Bruno was at home in Italy, especially in the company of four beautiful twenty-somethings and his own dear Bridget. Bridget loved the buzz at the table as the young women bubbled over with conversation.

As they ate and sipped, the four au pair friends shared insights about how the Italian families who employed them differed. One's family was religious, one extremely social, and another consisted of a single mother who, in the au pair's opinion, did a good job of spending time with her children and having a life of her own. Christine shared the comment of the Italian father who said that previously they had never thought of sending their children to the U.S. or Great Britain for education. Now, they think these English speaking countries might be a better place for young people to settle, so stalled was the Italian economy in 2013.

Bridget thought to herself, we are next if the Koch brothers have their way. It will be just like Berlusconi's rule.

The early spring days alternated between rainy and dry, but always cool. Bruno was a wiz at public transportation. Most fun of all was riding the trollies. Those in San Francisco were built in Milan. Bridget recalled being in San Francisco and seeing the word MILANO while riding a cable car up a steep incline. In Milan nobody hung off the sides of the cable car as it coursed through the flat center of town.

The weather was nippy, perfect for a stop for hot chocolate, which they found in a specialty shop serving only that. Just short of a pudding, the drink needed to be consumed with a spoon. The modern design of the store was a mixture of glass and steel. It was a nice contrast to the warm, dense treat.

Bridget was proud of all the walking that she was doing but, after six hours on her feet, she had to stop. Bruno could keep going forever and he did, never minding to go out for a bottle of wine or to study a train schedule while Bridget rested.

After Bridget revived they took in an exhibit of Modigliani and his contemporaries at the modern museum and later a food show at the design museum. They also made an appointment to see one of Milan's biggest treasures, DaVinci's *Last Supper*. Later they window-shopped in the high fashion district, taking photos of clothes and their unbelievably high prices. A summer dress and cardigan for a six-year-old girl cost $600!

Their week flew by. They felt lucky in their choice of hotel. It was thrilling to see Christine who would join them for Easter in Assisi.

 Virginia Salinsky Landgreen

Florence Revisited

On the day they left Milan for Florence, they walked from the subway to the train station. Bridget wheeled her suitcase through a few inches of snow. They left the white powder behind them as they watched from the train window. They were headed to the Santa Maria Novella train station, an example of Mussolini-era architecture. The bold lines of the transportation buildings were a backdrop for a group of statues of solidly built men and women devoid of romanticism or frill.

Ah, Firenze! They walked through the station to a familiar bus stop to head to Via Santo Spirito. Bridget had booked three nights in the Residenza d'Epoca which was not far from where they had rented an apartment for a month on three previous trips. She had discovered it online. They later noticed Residenze d'Epoca in Venice and Assisi.

The name is a marketing tool to denote 18th and 19th century Belle Époque buildings featuring furniture and furnishings of that era for travelers looking for a certain experience. Everything was in excellent repair. The furniture was finished with rich fabrics. The curtains were opulent too.

Luckily they had access across the hall to a kitchen even larger than the mini kitchen in their room. Bridget was fighting a cold and nothing tasted better than hot tea and plenty of it. It rained most of the three nights they were in Florence. In the mornings they would head to the nearby Trinità caffè for cappuccini, pastries or a panino. Bruno packed in a few more museums while Bridget recovered from her cold by sleeping.

They took advantage of an early spring day to walk through the Boboli Gardens and the neighboring, newly opened Villa Bardini Gardens, which had been under reconstruction for the last twenty years. Affected by the sheer beauty of the entrance to the Boboli, Bridget and Bruno stopped in their tracks and gave each other a long hug. They remembered what was ahead for them. Other visits had been in different seasons. This time early wildflowers popped up amid the fountains and statues.

Bridget and Bruno later enjoyed a very memorable meal at La Tarocca, a spot recommended by their friend Angela. They ordered a dish consisting of bundles of pear-filled pasta with gorgonzola white sauce over them. Each was tied with a fine strand of green onion, a true work of art.

On this visit they also had a lunch at the Mercato Centrale. They could never visit Florence without a little shopping and the famous boiled beef sandwich on a fresh hard roll, washed down with a glass of red jug wine.

Several times they returned to Bar Ricchi on Piazza Santo Spirito for an aperitivo or coffee, sharing happy memories of being there with family and friends. Friends reported that the Christmas before there was an evening of images projected onto the blank façade of the Basilica di Santo Spirito, Brunelleschi's renowned creation. When they entered the bar, Bruno and Bridget sat in the interior room where there were post cards showing the many projected images: Gucci's logo, the Mona Lisa, a snake, peace signs, and other whimsy.

They had spent more time in Florence than in any other Italian city, one month in each of the years 2001, 2003, and 2008. They had always rented the same apartment from friends, Lucy Lamp and David Lunn, who had formerly lived in Eugene. The apartment was on the third floor of a building built in the 1600's. It had two bedrooms, a spacious bathroom, a small kitchen, a dining area, and a comfortable living room with couches, chairs and satellite TV with channels from all around the world. Inside Bridget and Bruno's dream apartment were spectacular antiques, linens, plus many items from IKEA to make the small space both opulent and comfortable. The unit had no balconies or window boxes for flowers, but it had 10-foot ceilings with open beams and European style windows that adjusted six different ways.

Downstairs, just outside the apartment, was the piazza, which was ringed with trendy trattorias where locals and travelers dined al fresco under umbrellas when the weather permitted. Also, two of the most colorful bars were nestled in. Most of the buildings around the piazza were four stories high with commercial spaces on the ground floor. For centuries the area has been known for its artists and for the crafts being created there. The jewel and anchor of the open square was the Basilica di Santo Spirito.

Early in the mornings, when the song of starlings filled the air, parishioners would climb the stone steps to the church. It had been designed by Brunelleschi, who also designed the dome of the Duomo. Bridget, Bruno and occasional visitors spent time inside Santo Spirito and even more time sitting on the steps used by travelers for water breaks and picnics.

In the year of their first stay in the apartment (May of 2001), starting around midnight, revelers would break glass in the square until three in the morning. Bridget and Bruno soon learned that this was a nightly occurrence. By 6 a.m. a municipal worker would come and sweep it all up with a broom that looked like an upside-down tree. Bridget and Bruno got used to the sound, which they could hear if the windows were open. When they returned in 2003, they learned that glass had been outlawed on the steps.

To the left of the church entrance was the carabinieri station, where every native Florentine male, for decades, registered for service at eighteen.

Apparently throwing and breaking things was not unusual in Italy. In the 1960's it was traditional to throw chipped plates, broken glasses, and faulty objects out of the window on New Year's Day. There was even a report of a toilet bowl thrown out of a second story window (beware anyone walking underneath), again to be cleaned up by municipal workers.

Bridget learned from her son, Jaan, who in 2001 spent the most time out with the revelers who were on the steps, that young Italians had long been coming to this piazza to drink and carouse. He felt the bottle breaking had something to do with a protest to the recent gentrification that had gone on. The loud activity was joined with a spirit of anarchy in the new millennium. Jaan had even seen a picture of a well-known Eugene anarchist, Donald McConnald, in a flyer on a folding table set up during the varied daytime activities in the piazza. Later that summer, at the end of July in 2001, 300,000 demonstrators would gather in Genoa to rally against the G-8 Summit and globalization.

The piazza was a hub for the bohemian community known as Oltrano. It was across the Arno from the more touristy part of the city. A market would pop up every day from 8am to 3pm. One day there would be tables with vegetables from different farms and tables with bed linens and inexpensive clothing. Another day tables would be full of antiques, and on the next it would be items that were organic—food and home products. In the evening hours it was one of the trendiest spots in Florence to gather, whether on the steps of the church or in the bars and chic restaurants.

In 2001, Bruno and Bridget's first year in the apartment, a month had been given to them as a thank you for some glass work that Bruno had done for Lucy; they had only to pay for the weekly cleaning and utilities. In 2003 they paid 2,000 euros ($2,268) plus cleaning and utilities. In 2008 the price had doubled (4,000 euros) and the euro to dollar ratio was 1 euro equaled to $1.50, so the cost was $6,000 plus cleaning and utilities. As they were checking out the booking agent asked if they would be coming back. With chagrin, Bridget answered that she was afraid it was something they could no longer afford.

That year (2008), besides the daily adventures and wonderful meals often shared with guests, there had been an undercurrent. It was the year that Obama would be elected. It was a heated campaign. Sarah Palin entering the political scene as John McCain's running mate had put reason on tilt. Bush was leaving office and the U.S. was a hot mess. The saving grace was being in Italy and watching *Late Night with David Letterman*, and laughing about it because that was all you could do in September of 2008.

Also, that last visit was a time of repairs and reconstruction in the condo. Occasionally a worker would bang on the third story kitchen window and climb through it from the scaffolding to use the bathroom or get a drink of water. Italians are very patient with reconstruction and restoration projects and Bridget and Bruno did their best to take this like Italians. In addition, workmen were repairing the *facciata* (the outer surface) of the building. From 8 a.m. until 3 p.m. there was loud chiseling and hacking of the stone in the light well outside the kitchen window.

Revisiting the nearby trattoria, *Casalinga* (the Housewife), for lunch and dinners was a counterbalance to anything less than perfect. This was a real touchstone where they had shared many meals, over their visits, with family and friends. It was full of locals and the wait staff hadn't changed much in a decade. The food was classic, simple, and fresh.

In 2011, Bridget noticed more people in Italy wearing jeans since their first visit. The older people (now their peers) were often in stylish workout clothes plus fashionable or impeccable outfits. There was still the same bustle of individuals sharing the narrow sidewalks or traveling by bike or scooter through the streets, where art presents itself at every blink of the eye.

From that first visit in 2001, walking and living in Florence was life-changing for Bridget. It was, for her, like hearing opera for the first time. She sensed she was watching fashion made real on every Italian she saw. She came home, sold her house in the woods, bought a two-bedroom condo with no balcony, and began to reduce possessions to fit into their new footprint.

And she began to plan for their return. In 2003 they would spend a month traveling in France and a month living in the apartment. Bridget and Bruno would make more trips in the future to other places in Italy.

Their three days in Florence passed quickly in the spring visit of 2011. When they were at the Santa Maria Novella station, ready for their next destination, it was Bridget's job to watch Bruno's back as he purchased their tickets from the machine. She had to shout, "*FERMA, FERMA!*" (stop) fiercely to the Roma woman who was trying to distract her by offering to help them use the machine to buy train tickets. The woman's accomplice hovered nearby looking for pockets to pick. Disaster averted! Tourists are frequently caught off guard when they are absorbed in the complexities of ticket purchasing. Bruno and Bridget left the rain behind them, boarded the train and headed to their next stop.

"Goodbye, Firenze" whispered Bridget, feeling a mixture of sadness and anticipation.

Assisi

Bridget and Bruno's apartment in Assisi, near the San Rufino cathedral, was familiar and spacious. Just two years before, they had spent eleven days there. They happily accommodated the guests who visited.

Bruno's stepdaughter Rosaria and her traveling partner Dan arrived for three nights. Soon the apartment was strewn with wet wool clothes and laundry. Their visit was part of a much longer trip in Europe. Bridget and Bruno had not met Dan before and since Rosaria had been living with him in California for three years, they welcomed this chance to see them.

Rosaria, a dark-haired beauty and a head-turner, and Bruno were able to take a few long walks. Bridget appreciated how special these times were since, for her, being alone with her grown children Jaan and Sarina was sheer delight. One evening the party, including Mara and Luigi, returned to the restaurant La Rocca because, Bridget and Mara agreed, it is the best place to eat in Assisi. Bridget also had longed for the onion pizza from the corner shop, "da Andrea," since their last visit and she was excited to share this fresh take on the all vegetable specialty. Time flew by and soon the young couple were packed and off on their adventure.

Once again Bridget and Bruno observed the gathering at San Rufino before the Easter procession. A single file of robed clergy traveled from the top of the town's highest church to the bottom near the extra large Basilica of San Francesco. It was a magnificent sight to see the tall torches light the way in the dark during the procession. A drummer sounding a single beat on a base drum, echoing a heartbeat, led the way. The town is dedicated to San Francesco (Francis) and his followers. In it, the art of Giotto and the poetry of Dante have highlighted the life of this extraordinary man. Many tourists and pilgrims find this destination one with sacred overtones. The event moved Bridget. She wondered if her dreams would be full of angels.

The next day Bridget and Bruno shared the Easter feast with old and new friends. The city of pink and white stone was bursting with spring flowers from windows and balconies. Christine, their young friend from Eugene whom they had met at the beginning of their trip, visited from Milan. She was a delight to be with and they all enjoyed touring the town. During her short stay the town was frosted with a confection of light snow.

And then it struck, as it had on her six previous trips. Right on time. Three weeks in came the homesickness. Bridget longed to be back in Oregon, where walking around town was not always uphill, where she usually had some idea of where she was unlike never having a mental map of Assisi, and where she could load up on supplies. Where the flannel sheets would not pop up from the mattress, and where she could make soups and stews from things she had on hand to gird against the rain. In Oregon, green shimmered from tree trunk to tree-top in the spring. She could slip a bike ride in between the rain showers, wearing fewer and fewer layers of clothing as the weather warmed. The lambs were lambing and she would see them in the emerald fields since surely she would be driving back and forth to Portland to see her daughter Sarina and son-in-law John and to hold her granddaughter Gemma in her arms. Bridget was one of two helping grandmothers. She longed not for buildings built in stone in the 12th century but for words written in stone by her fellow Oregonians. In the center of Eugene on the downtown square are Ken Kesey's opening lines to his book *Sometimes a Great Notion*.

> *"Along the western slopes of the Oregon*
> *Costal Range...come look: the hysterical*
> *crashing of the tributaries as they merge*
> *into...the Wakonda Auga River..."*

She thought of Cecelia Hagen's poem on a wall in the Kaiser Westside Center in Hillsboro, Oregon, at the elevator landing:

> *"Every rock comes from a mountain. It breaks loose,*
> *tumbles free, and now this one resting in my palm."*

Bridget missed her sister Anna, who was probably doing a lot of tango dancing, and the centering talks they had as they prepared their garden for planting each spring. She also missed the patterns that she and Bruno had chosen for their lives: the walks downtown, reading the local newspaper silently in the mornings, and watching PBS news in the evenings.

She felt grumpy and weepy and all she wanted to do was stay inside and watch Italian TV or read. She didn't have the energy for long walks in the cold or any desire to view another church. Assisi had numerous beautiful churches and many beautiful buildings. Bruno continued to explore.

And then one morning Bridget woke to find that the homesickness had passed, as it always did. She could wholeheartedly resume the great gift of travel in Italy. Mara, Luigi, Bridget and Bruno borrowed a friend's car and traveled to Todi, the town that was recognized by Time magazine in the late 90's as the most livable city in the world. Bridget and Bruno were shocked to find many empty storefronts. It stood like a ghost town, to the chagrin of the few remaining shopkeepers. How could this happen? Maybe because it was difficult to get to Todi without a car? It had no religious shrines or museums to lure pilgrims. The investors who moved to Todi in its heyday bought large properties outside of the city center and did their shopping at businesses outside of Todi, near their homes.

The sadness Bridget felt as they walked the strangely empty streets reignited her quest to understand Italy. She began on a search to uncover what had gone on to cause Todi to slip away after being the once great city of the 1990's. Her curiosity helped her move beyond missing her familiar Oregon.

Because they grew to know Assisi so well, Bridget and Bruno's three weeks offered an opportunity to feel a bit like expatriates. They again borrowed Mara's friend's car and drove to nearby towns to shop in supermarkets or open air markets. Bridget and Bruno attended free cultural events and discovered some small museums they had not known of before.

By the time they hugged Mara Gattara good-bye and thanked her for her kindness and hospitality, Bridget was ready for the next adventure.

Trieste

When they left Assisi, it was a full day of train travel to reach Trieste in the northeastern corner of Italy. Both Bruno and Bridget were delighted by the warmer days with blue sky and the sunny disposition of all the Triestini they met. This beautiful sea town was where James Joyce came to write *Portrait of the Artist as a Young Man*. The influence of the Hapsburgs was everywhere in the architecture. In this city of trade, the large buildings were of a different era and scale than what they had visited so far in Italy. The historic town palazzo was the biggest they had seen, and it looked out onto the Adriatic. They stayed three nights in the large hotel near the train station and felt energized by each new discovery. One was that the folks around them enjoyed an aperitivo early in the afternoon. Nowhere had they seen such a great variety of cicchetti included with a drink. There were tiny sandwiches, olives, rice balls, and the usual nuts and chips.

Bridget and Bruno toured the home of a shipping merchant who had financed the building of the Suez Canal. It had many treasures in the public rooms. The opera *Aida* was commissioned to commemorate the opening of the canal. There was a museum nearby with an exhibit documenting this cultural event. The neighboring modern art museum displayed sculptures by contemporary artists and paintings created in the last century.

It was a luxury to be in their Trieste hotel room, which had a plush quality that their apartment in Assisi lacked. The shower had several options for spray. The towels were fluffy. The toiletries were abundant and the TV could be watched from bed. Their breakfast was included and was geared to travelers like Bridget who loved eggs and bacon in the morning. Bruno was happy with a cappuccino and a cornetto. They were by now used to the matron (a standard fixture in some Italian hotels) whose job it was to make sure that nobody left the dining room with a banana stuffed away for later.

When they left Trieste they traveled by bus through Slovenia to Croatia, where they had arranged to rent an apartment in the sea town of Rovinj for a week. Bridget was reluctant to leave Italy. On a short trip to Switzerland, six years earlier, she couldn't get back across the border to Italy fast enough. The stern nature of the people she met on that brief trip was a sharp contrast to the warm, jovial Italians she loved. Neither of them had any idea of what to expect from Croatia.

Also, Bridget had resisted travel into Eastern Europe because she felt she could eat all of the cabbage and potatoes that she wanted at home. Still, they had been lured by tales of an architecture that was said to be like that of Venice and an economy that resembled Italy's before it joined the European Union. As they traveled by bus through a narrow slice of Slovenia, they saw vineyard after vineyard and many brick farmhouses. They listened to the people on the bus chat in a language that was not musical like Italian. There were mostly older women, and their figures had spread much like Bridget's had. Half of Bridget's DNA came from Eastern Europe.

They were greeted at the bus stop by their host who helped load their luggage into his van. He drove them through the small town to the top of the hill where their apartment was in a very pleasant neighborhood in the same building as their young landlord and his family. He was careful to point out the supermarket nearby, which would become a landmark and also a handy source of food and wine.

Croatia

Bridget had never been this far east in Europe. Twenty years earlier there had been war in Bosnia and Herzegovina, Slovenia, Serbia, Montenegro, Macedonia, and Croatia, all of which had been parts of Yugoslavia when Bridget was growing up. The coastline of Croatia on the Adriatic Sea, from south of Rijeka to south of Dubrovnik, had been under siege. Almost 70% of Dubrovnik's buildings were shelled. Even today, landmines are lurking in the impoverished, inland countries of this region.

Bridget and Bruno's landlord and his pretty wife, parents of boys ages ten and twelve, showed them which bikes, from among the tangle in the garage, would be best for them to use. Bridget and Bruno's arrival in early May was ahead of the families who would arrive when school was out. Come summer, every room in Rovinj would be rented to visitors who enjoyed this beautiful town on the sea. Then the bike rack and all the bikes would be put outside for rentals.

The landlord Alberto, in near perfect English, showed them how to operate things in the apartment. There was a handy clothes washer, a TV with satellite coverage, and European style windows and doors that tilted as well as moved up and down. Alberto gave them keys and confessed that no one ever locked doors in this town. When he adjusted the TV to English-speaking news, Bridget and Bruno learned of the Boston Marathon bombing.

They were horrified and shaken as they made a meal of some items they had picked at the supermarket. Prices were very much less than in Italy or even the U.S. They drank wine, ate sardines from a can, and had cheese, cured meat, and bread as they followed the news from the states.

What a horrible tragedy to happen in the middle of a large vulnerable crowd. Bridget had never been in a war. She had never even fired a gun. The world seemed a precarious place these days; natural disasters were on the rise, too.

Bridget felt lucky but ultra-cautious at every turn and step, which was getting on Bruno's nerves. Still, at 64 years old she considered herself more than robust to be managing without a car for two months. She simply ignored Bruno sometimes. She knew that they wouldn't even have been on this trip without her planning and budgeting. Even though she never did get her bearings during the week they were in Rovinj, she felt no guilt for depending on Bruno for leading their "tour of two" and being the IT specialist along the way.

Early the next morning, after checking email and news, they took the bikes out for a first adventure. The apartment was advertised as being a ten-minute walk from the center of town, which faced the Adriatic and contained good cafés and restaurants. Their ride to town was downhill and consisted of many switchbacks. As she kept her eye on the uneven pavement and the traffic, Bridget realized that she had been spoiled by bike lanes back home.

Even Bruno was lost a few times as they cycled back and forth, up and down between the center of town and their apartment. Eventually they took the park road, which led to a handy bike path around the waterfront. This was a more circuitous and breathtaking route.

Every hundred yards there would be a building looking like it was from the WPA era. Most of these places had signs that said they would be open in a week or so. When opened, they would serve seafood and beverages.

Most of the restaurants in town were open. Wait staff, starched and formal, were standing in front searching for the crowd that was nowhere in sight. Some of the small shops were setting up for the tourists. Bridget had read about, but never before seen, a mani-pedi shop where little fish would nibble away the dead skin from around toes. It would open later. They passed a champagne bar that they had seen on a Rick Steves episode featuring Croatia. The drinks were served out on the rocks, where underwater lights created a unique experience. Unfortunately they never made it back to town when it was dark. Just knowing it was there, however, made Bridget happy.

The main cathedral, St. Euphemia, was on the highest point overlooking the sea and the rock walls of various heights. Bruno and Bridget watched in awe as a small wedding party took photographs on flat rocks that stretched out into the Adriatic. The bride and groom were dressed formally, the bride in a long white wedding dress and veil, the groom in black tie. Two bridesmaids wore floor length dresses of pale peach and joined two groomsmen, also in black tie. The photographer snapped away as the wedding party struck different poses.

Beside the church was a lovely café, a sight which Bridget was fond of seeing everywhere in their travels. If it is in Europe and is interesting to visit, then it is worthy of some refreshment in a beautiful setting to heighten the experience.

They parked their bikes and explored the narrow streets of the old town. Earlier they had passed large quarries, the source of the famous Istrian stone used to build the streets and buildings of Venice. It wasn't surprising, then, to see similar styles of buildings in the old town.

A woman and her daughter who were setting up their restaurant invited Bruno and Bridget inside to sample her grappa. Grappa is fire water made from the pulp and stems after grapes are pressed for wine. After sampling five flavors, Bruno settled on a bottle. They traveled to the open market for fresh vegetables and fish which they purchased and added to their backpacks. Bridget bought some truffle pesto from a woman from Kosovo who had a desperate look in her eye. Though she knew they would love the pesto, Bridget made her purchase more out of sympathy.

They unlocked their bikes and began the uphill ride home. Because they had taken a few different routes back and forth to their apartment Bridget never was sure where they were. The ride was steep. She never felt safe in traffic even though there wasn't a lot. She questioned Bruno, who was riding up ahead, about their location since it seemed like they had been riding long enough to be home. Bruno reluctantly agreed that they were lost. They asked a passing driver in a car for directions and got on the right path back to the apartment. Bridget's fondness for bike riding was fading for the day.

When she got home and saw 90.00 on the jar she couldn't believe she would have spent 90 euros ($130.00) on just a jar of pesto. Then she realized that it was the local currency kuna, not euros, and she had spent more like $7.00. They added truffle pesto to many dishes, including pasta, and it was delicious.

One day Bridget and Bruno traveled by bus to Pula, a town that still had Greek and Roman ruins. They admired the buildings and found their way to the open air market. In addition to the beautiful meats and vegetables, there were small, modest lunch stalls. Bridget couldn't wait to order a plate of sardines. She had always been a fan of sardines and remembered eating them with her mother when she was growing up. When they arrived the sardines were large and had bones which were not hard to pick out. Bridget enjoyed them immensely.

Another day, back in Rovinj, they splurged for tickets on a sightseeing boat. A ticket salesman welcomed them while hawking this adventure to everyone who passed by. Bridget and Bruno settled on board with four other small family groups. A large man who was the host on the boat's "team" offered everyone a grappa. "Good to settle your stomach on the water, good for your health, and good for your nerves. Good for everything," he added. Little convincing was needed.

Right before their eyes a man roared onto the dock on his motorbike, hopped off, and jumped onboard. He was the ship's captain, appearing a bit like a rabbit coming out of a black hat!

The wind picked up out on the water. The other family groups had young children and they snuggled together to stay warm. Bruno and Bridget were dressed warmly and sat as close to each other as possible. The member of the crew who had offered them the grappa pointed out the marina and resorts along the way. There was so much undeveloped land on the shore that it reminded Bridget of Oregon. Much of nature was preserved.

The coast was spectacular and during the rest of their week in Croatia Bridget and Bruno were able to visit some of the spots they had spied from the boat including a section of town with some beautiful old homes.

Croatia was an enjoyable country to visit, a perfect spot on the sea. It was a grand adventure. All of the residents whom they met were aware of the Boston Marathon bombing and sympathetic, gracious, and also happy that the tourist season was about to begin.

Venice

After their week in Croatia, Bruno and Bridget had plans to spoil themselves further with a week in the city on the water. Venice, more than any other place in her beloved Italy, held magic for Bridget. She had read mystery novels by Donna Leon set in Venice, and watched the German TV series of those novels that were filmed on location. All of this whetted her appetite for her fourth trip to Venice.

With high expectations they arrived by train on a rainy grey morning. They set off by vaporetto to disembark at the Fondamente Nove stop, where they had arranged to meet their landlord, Christian. He would show them the apartment they would take over for the week of their visit. The waterbus ride did not disappoint Bridget. Was it her favorite thing to do? Possibly.

Bruno had purchased passes for the week, so she knew there would be countless rides ahead. They boarded with their luggage and stayed on the upper deck until some seats down the small flight of stairs were available. Each vaporetto had two seats on the bottom level reserved for people traveling with large parcels or luggage. Bridget's eyes overflowed with happy tears as they viewed the sights.

There were seven stops on the canal before reaching theirs. The waterscape was familiar, a most welcome sight to her.

It was a long haul from their vaporetto stop to their new apartment, and especially so with luggage. It was garbage pick-up day and what looked like haphazard arrangements of plastic bags overflowing with garbage were hung from most doors or were propped inside doorways. Bridget and Bruno would soon find that Venetians followed a very strict protocol for recycling certain items on certain days of the week. Everything had to be transported on and off the island by boat.

Christian was young and handsome and told them with pride that he was a fourth generation Veneziano. When Bridget complimented him on the appearance of the apartment, he laughed and credited his father, an anthropologist. His, he said, was all white and modern. The apartment had a series of beautifully framed primitive drawings of animals. The walls and furniture were of natural hues, and the apartment was efficiently laid out on the second of three floors of the narrow, vertical building that shared walls with buildings on either side, as do most buildings on Venetian streets. On a map he pointed out a favorite bar in the neighborhood and the grocery market. He then took their official document information, explained the use of the apartment, and left.

Once they settled in and checked their email, they set out to explore, following the zig-zag of the streets that they thought led away from the canal, only to find themselves at the canal again, and at the doorway to the small bar that Christian had recommended. It was 4:00 by now, a respectable aperitivo hour. The bar had standing room only, since all three of the small tables were full. The rain had stopped, people spilled out of the bar, *Ponte Rosso*, balancing plates of seafood (mussels, grande gamberetti, calamari) and glasses of wine on the ancient steps that led to the red bridge over the neighborhood waterway.

Bruno moved up to the bar to read the menu and inquired in Italian about an item. A handsome grey-haired patron replied in Italian, and before long they had traded enough information to reveal that Bruno's new Italian friend not only knew where Oregon was, he had seen a video of "la Veneta," the Oregon Country Fair, and his favorite band, The Grateful Dead! This commonality prompted him to buy a round of Campari spritz for Bruno and Bridget. Their new friend offered that his favorite song of the band was *Uncle John's Band*. Bruno explained that he had sold his fused glass at the Oregon Country Fair for forty years. This caused the couple to become famous for 15 seconds.

Their friend introduced himself as a fourth generation gondolier. His wife and he had one child, a girl, who was a pharmacist. He offered to give them a free ride in the morning, a very generous notion (rides cost between $35-$200 per person), but they felt they had to decline. Then he introduced Bruno and Bridget to the man standing next to him, also a glass artist, who bought them another round of aperitivi.

The two glass artists talked about their trade and famous artists they had worked with or known (with Bridget adding as many of her few Italian phrases as possible to the lively chatter). Eventually Bridget and Bruno left, finding their way home with some difficulty in the maze of still unfamiliar streets and bridges. Everything looked different in the waning light. They would return to Ponte Rosso for drinks and a meal three more times before leaving Venice, and had to agree with their landlord: this was a most enchanting neighborhood bar.

Waking up in their new location after a light meal and a sound night's sleep, Bruno and Bridget were ready for adventure. After a bit of coffee, made at home in the *caffetteria* (typical Italian vacuum espresso maker), they headed off for their vaporetto stop. Bridget discovered a café behind the platform, perfect for a panini, an espresso shot, and a bathroom break. This became another place that they popped in and visited frequently during their stay. It was a typical bar, serving light meals and food to take away from the wrap-around showcase under the bar.

Their vaporetto traveled under a grey sky across choppy water to the stop in front of the Danieli Royal Excelsior Hotel, where many gondolas were moored, ready to ease travelers through the by-ways of the canals. They saw the sign they had been looking for, *Gondole Danieli*. This was a very posh part of the canal for visitors. It looked like gondola central because of all of the activity around the water.

Bridget spotted their friend from the night before. He was clearly off duty, wearing a nylon wind breaker over his iconic horizontally striped polo shirt. The gondoliers are known for their good looks and strong physiques and their silver haired acquaintance was no exception. They greeted each other warmly, and he was kind enough to pose with them for a photo. He did not repeat his offer of the complimentary gondola ride, which Bridget and Bruno understood had been made in a moment of rash enthusiasm. Subdued under the morning light, they left the gondola stop and walked into the center of town to the famous opera house, La Fenice. They bought tickets to tour the building, built in 1792. Teatro La Fenice had burned twice and was nearly destroyed in the second fire of 1996. It was turned over to the community and restored in 2003.

The lobby was elegant, white and golden-hued. Large clear crystal chandeliers hung above and two ten-step staircases led to the theatre. Bridget imagined grandly dressed Venetians and world travelers rubbing elbows before a performance.

The theatre overflowed with Baroque splendor. Bridget and Bruno were guided to a theatre box (seats for 8 people) and watched a rehearsal for Mozart's *Don Giovanni* on the famous stage.

For Bridget, this was another near-perfect experience. No need to buck a crowd or put on dress clothes. The performers, too, were in their street clothes. She admired the command of the maestro, Antonello Manacorda, at the podium. Stage blockers and the lighting crew worked amidst the artists. It was so rewarding to see opera in the making. Bridget, a theatre arts undergraduate major, had spent many days in her college theatre preparing like this. Those days were some of the happiest times of her life.

The set, designed by Paolo Fantin, rotated 360 degrees. The indoor scenes had very tall ceilings. It was possible for the opera to be staged in two rooms of the set at once, although that was not always what the script called for. There were to be eight performances, with several cast members sharing the major parts. The tenor they saw rehearsing was young and very handsome. The action on stage was passionate. At one point the young soprano's bodice (even in street clothes) was ripped by Don Giovanni to reveal her bare breast!

The two travelers spent an hour watching the rehearsal. They were not hurried, but the docents kept an eagle eye on them to make sure they did not film or in any way interrupt the rehearsal. When performed, *Don Giovanni* is a 3-½ hour production.

On the way out of the opera house, the pair passed the large, elegant café where as much prosecco as coffee as served. They went in search of a more modest place for lunch. Nearby, they lucked into a modern restaurant that had large black-and-white photos from famous movie scenes on the walls. Many were American, which seemed a bit jolting but reminded them of the fine movie culture back home, one of the things they could be proud of. They spotted Marilyn Monroe, James Dean, and Frank Sinatra, among others. The servers were generous, bringing them extra baskets of potato chips and bread with their order. It was a popular place with locals and the conversations around them were lively. After lunch they strolled through Piazza San Marco.

Piazza San Marco is among the most beautiful outdoor spaces in the world. It faces the canal, is flanked by the famous Basilica of St. Mark and formal dining rooms with outside seating (weather permitting). Although the piazza was barely populated at noon, the restaurants' wait staffs stood ready, dressed in formal uniforms as starched as the white tablecloths. No matter what the weather in the grand "outdoor room," you can always count on a devoted flock of pigeons watching the tourists, hoping for crumbs, ready for a photo opportunity. San Marco is the only piazza in Venice. The other smaller piazza-like spaces throughout the city are called *campi* (literally "fields").

After taking in the sights, Bridget and Bruno returned to their apartment by vaporetto. It was already beginning to feel like home. Bridget took a rest while Bruno roamed the streets and visited as many places on his long list as he could.

When Bruno returned, they wandered out into the neighborhood together. They found a table in the nearby campo surrounding the famous church Chiesa di San Giovanni e Paolo and watched the parents visit with each other as the children, who all seemed to be under 7, played with balls or practiced riding on bikes. This was the local park, although it had no grass. The canal marked the out-of-bounds area for soccer balls. Bruno ordered them drinks and snacks before heading home for a salad and an early evening of Italian TV.

The next morning Bridget woke up to find herself in a foul mood. This was unusual for her. Maybe it had something to do with the bizarre dreams she was having, and often had, when she traveled. To her, it wasn't a bad trade off to have all the bad happen during sleep time, leaving the waking hours to be calm and relatively happy. But this morning her bad dream about missing flights and trains left a lingering feeling that lasted through breakfast and left her with a bit of melancholy.

Lately she had noticed that she could go from zero to ten rapidly when she got angry. Perhaps it was her waning hormones as she approached her 65th birthday. She had lived year after year with a steady good humor, so maybe a few dips and peaks could be tolerated. She knew it was important to make her needs and wants known, to express her feelings. If they were always the same (general acceptance of all things and people), it could become a dulling experience for those around her. She would rather communicate her genuine feelings.

When they traveled in Italy, where wine and spirits were inexpensive, Bridget had to carefully watch not to overdo it. Opening a second bottle of wine guaranteed a slow, foggy morning, giving Bruno a good reason to walk two steps ahead of her, as he generally did. "Does he think he's in Japan?" she sometimes fumed to herself. There was no keeping up with Bruno in Italy, where he wanted to see so many things and she wanted to take in each sight and savor it.

It was true that Bridget had put on weight in the last 20 years. She had always been slender as an adult but now, with the additional pounds she was a large (she liked to think "robust") woman. A man living in her high-rise at home had called her "stacked," an old fashioned phrase. The Italians would use the phrase *abbondante*.

Still, she exercised regularly and prided herself on her endurance during their travels. Luckily, her joints were not giving out yet, and she was dedicated to her gentle yoga practice and gym classes back at home. She was not too wrinkled, but she knew it was coming. She didn't plan to do much about it, either, besides getting the occasional facial and wearing sunscreen. She was diligent about taking her supplements. She and Bruno ate huge salads often, and made desserts a rare treat.

Bruno was still trim. His hairline had receded—she knew because she was his barber—but he was aging well. He was self-conscious about his double chin, a family characteristic which appeared more as the years advanced.

This was the first time Bridget had traveled with a laptop computer. She was able to stay in touch with friends and family back home by email and post pictures and details of their experiences. In spite of this increased contact she missed her sister, Anna, and their easy talks in the garden or while walking. And she missed her grown children, their partners and their granddaughter, Gemma.

Not counting her recent morning of grouchiness, Bridget was generous and patient most of the time. She had reached the level of accountability and integrity that comes with age. Without being matronly, she had become a matron.

She would not call herself a Christian, because she could easily adopt the values in many spiritual practices. However, she enjoyed the rituals involved within her Episcopalian place of worship and the cultural events surrounding the seasons. Bridget felt right at home in the many churches in Italy that she and Bruno visited; he went for the art and architecture and she for the feeling of hundreds of years of parishioners bringing their hearts and their lives to be uplifted.

As the number of days they had left in Venice dwindled, so did Bridget's spirit. She and Bruno tried to fill each moment with unexpected sights and visits to new destinations. There was the trip by vaporetto to the dramatic dome of Longhena's Chiesa di Santa Maria della Salute, where they saw an art installation that took over an entire palazzo. An oriental carpet design had been photographed and reproduced on every wall of every room of the palace. In addition, the artist had done several very abstract 6 foot by 6 foot oil paintings in shades of charcoal. Another room with wall coverings of the same carpet design had a contrasting photo of a man reproduced in oils (shades of gray) in the same 6 foot by 6 foot scale. The paintings were hung on the patterned walls. Bridget loved it and made a note to paint some of their interior walls grey when they returned home.

Once outside the palace, Bridget watched an older gentleman who sat playing the violin as he looked out over the water. He squatted, leaning his back against the building that stood on the most outlying tip of the island. Was he thinking of a lost love as he played his melancholy song? Seeing him made Bridget think of her granddaughter Gemma back home, who was studying the violin. It also reminded her that she and Bruno would soon be leaving Venice.

They went by vaporetto to another part of the island that they had yet to explore. Then they walked through the Jewish quarter (just five minutes away from San Paolo) as they had many times before. They marveled at its contrasts of very luxurious hotels and very impoverished dwellings. The neighborhood, also called the ghetto, is famous for its food.

There was a photographic exhibit at Tre Oci Gallery by Gianni Berengo Gardin, who had produced over 200 books of photographs from all over the world. The photos enthralled her. He organized his work around significant dates: pre-World War I, post-World War II and the 1960's. He photographed people in major cities around the world with a focus on Italy and the U.S. Bridget loved the art of photographers who bring a sense of energy with the changing times to their work.

After viewing the exhibit, they rode the vaporetto as far as it would go, first this way, then that way. They visited the Lido, which is off the lagoon and accessible by car since it is on the mainland, and bought groceries for their last meals. Then came the final night and the final meal out, which they selected with great care. Bruno had seafood pasta and Bridget had liver and onions, a specialty in Venice.

Was it because there were no cars that defined a certain pace of travel? Was it because Venice is a magnet for culture and has been a jewel for so long? Was the vapor that rose from the lagoon an aphrodisiac? For Bridget, the answer to the question of where was her favorite place in Italy would always be Venice, with Bruno: She couldn't navigate there without him.

Of course, she was crazy about Bruno. Their late-in-life romance had come after a series of marriages which failed to prosper for either of them. It was either give up or throw the dice one more time. This time she got lucky…snake eyes.

And also, wide-open eyes…for both of them. They had loved and lost before. They felt like teenagers that first year of their relationship back in Eugene and missed several appointments because the urge to jump into bed together won out. Now, after two decades, they felt like well-matched people of their own age. The passion was still there, and it had aged in a good way as well.

They packed and cleaned the apartment where they had spent the last week. They walked to the train and traveled 2-½ hours to the mountains. Bruno would introduce Bridget to his high school exchange student from Italy, Massimo, now Dr. Massimo Antonioli. Bruno had visited Massimo and his wife, Amelia, once before since those days of his youth.

Riding in the train, Bridget remembered that ride by vaporetto at 4:00 in the morning on an earlier visit, when she and Bruno were traveling from Murano, where they had stayed, to the train station to begin their journey back to Oregon. They had been the only people on the water taxi. Bruno wrapped his arms around her as they stood at the railing and rode down the Grand Canal. They rode passed Ca'Rezzonico (one of the larger palaces on the canal) designed by Longhena. The rose-colored glass in the lights on the canal matched the colors of the sky. There was no darkness in the early morning, and the quiet intensified each moment. They watched the palazzi leave their view. They both realized they might never see anything like this again.

Rovereto

Bruno and Bridget would visit the small town of Rovereto for two nights. They settled into their comfortable hotel which was not far from the train station and explored the *centro storico* (historic center) before meeting up with Massimo and Amelia, who then walked them to their home in an apartment. It was lovely. Each room was full of books. There was a large well-equipped kitchen (U.S. scale). It was obvious that they enjoyed both food and cooking. Amelia had retired from her practice as an internist to project-manage medical conferences and Massimo was a practicing psychiatrist.

As they had Campari spritz and were watching a meal of risotto with asparagus and tender veal being prepared, Amelia mentioned that, since it was Monday night, *Montalbano* would be on TV. Bruno and Bridget had enjoyed following the show, set in Sicily, during their travels. According to the reports, most households in Italy were tuned into the detective series. Bruno said they loved the show! Massimo laughed as he shared his earlier thoughts: the only thing not perfect about their visit was that they would be missing Monday's show. "PERFECTO!" said Amelia.

After the lovely home-cooked meal the two couples watched the TV show while sharing a few shots of grappa.

The next day the travelers amused themselves with the local stores and museums until Massimo and Amelia were done with their workday. They were whisked out of town and up into the Dolomite mountains where they visited a tavern where Massimo and Amelia liked to dine. It was only a thirty minute drive. Massimo would sometimes perform there with his rock and roll band *Nero Vinile* (Black Vinyl).

Tonight the entertainment was a rockabilly group. Bridget was delighted to see the Italian take on the American form. The spry standup bass player literally climbed to the neck of his base and played in the most outrageous way. They were great!

The next day the couples met and walked to the train station. They said their goodbyes, but not for long. A few days later they would meet briefly at the top of Lago di Garda. Bridget and Bruno were off to Desenzano, another lakeside town, for a week. This would be the last stop of their extravagant two month adventure.

Lago Di Garda

Bridget and Bruno traveled by train and bus to arrive in Desenzano del Garda. Bridget was thrilled to be greeted by their jovial host, Lorenzo, a man about their age. He helped load their modest amount of luggage into his utilitarian car, then drove them across the small town and up the hill to their apartment. Bridget least enjoyed this part of traveling—getting from public transportation to their rentals. It was always further than expected with unfamiliar surroundings and challenges. In the directions given by each hotel or owner it always said, "Just ten minutes from the train station by foot." That was never true and it was always at least thirty to forty minutes.

The week would be spent in a new building (three apartments) next door to an older house which Lorenzo also rented out. He explained with pride that his mother had lived in the house until she died.

Because they were preseason, Lorenzo had upgraded their apartment to one with a bath on the ground floor, where there was a kitchen and small lounge area, and also a full bath upstairs, where their bedroom was. There was a second sleep area loft above their bedroom. All was clean and comfortable. There was a jumble of bikes outside which they could use, but no helmets or locks were in sight. Bridget was beginning to prefer walking if hills were involved. Desenzano del Garda, like Rovinj, Croatia, was a town that sloped down gradually to the water.

Bruno had chosen this spot on Lago di Garda because it was a hub for the ferry routes. Situated at the southern end of the lake, they would have access to all of the stops along the way for day trips. On the weekend at the very end of their trip they would meet Massimo and Amelia in the town at the northern tip, Riva del Garda.

The older part of Desanzano bordered the lake. Large three-story hotels and places to eat (many tables with umbrellas) circled the waterfront. It was early in the season yet the shops were full, forecasting a busy summer for vacationers. Bridget was always happy when she was by water. They explored the shops and cafés and settled on a casual place for some panini and a glass of wine. A small *fruttovendolo* (vegetable and basics) storefront between the water and their apartment made it easy for them to pick up eggs, bread, cheese, vegetables, and wine the many times they climbed home after their excursions.

Five years previously they had stayed on Lago di Como, off-season, and remembered how delightful it was. Their accommodations were modest and charming. The towns are a little fancier on lake Como, and Bruno and Bridget were surprised by Lago di Garda's affordable rates, especially pre-season. They took in the sights of this most northern lake with its increasingly dramatic rocky cliffs. The buildings reflected simple bold lines to ward off the winters. Less was defined by decoration and more by the stalwart design, surrounded by snow-capped Alps blocking the setting sun and causing darkness to fall early in the afternoon.

The travelers settled into their routines—strong coffee in the morning followed by eggs at home or the search for the freshest crema cornetta. Bridget liked a panino in the morning. One afternoon, she made a server's mouth drop to the floor when she ordered her aperitivo with Cynar in it rather than Campari. "No, no, no! Cynar is a digestivo, no aperitivo," said the woman with disbelief and disdain. Bridget smiled as the drink was served to her.

One day they set out for a day trip by ferry to nearby Sirmione. A fascinating medieval castle, the Rocca Scaligera, is on the water with a moat filled with water from the lake. Bridget saw more wildlife on the water as they traveled than she had dreamed. The usual swifts, swallows and house martins were everywhere. Great reed warblers were seen around the small reedbeds as they pulled away from the tourist filled town. She thought she had seen a hoopoe and would check when she got home. They arrived back at their apartment in time to make dinner and watch Italian TV.

Garda is the largest lake in Italy, and Bridget and Bruno ended up spending hours traversing Lake Garda on the ferry. This was just fine with Bridget as she spied purple herons in the air. She observed the other travelers who were in families, couples and small groups. They rarely saw others from the U.S. They would find the sunny part of the boat and enjoy fresh mountain air. They always had the coastline to mark their progress. Lovely small towns accented the wild, green shore. It reminded Bridget of the San Juan Islands in British Columbia where she had visited two decades before. The concessions on the ferry were not yet operating to serve beverages and snacks but you could see that they were on a large enough scale to do a good business in the summer. Lake Garda, the most popular of the lakes, attracts seven percent of all the tourists who come to Italy and serves as a bridge between the Alps and the rest of the country.

They would alternate between a day in Desenzano and a day trip with a ferry loop to several towns. The last weekend they took their longest trip boarding early in the morning and arriving in Riva del Garda in the afternoon. There they met with Massimo and Amelia, who had only a twenty-five minute drive from their home Rovereto. Both Massimo and Amelia in their early years as physicians lived in Riva del Garda as newlyweds. Bridget and Bruno could feel their shared nostalgia as they walked around during the afternoon.

Massimo pointed out the upscale men's clothing store where he had surrendered to all of the salesman's suggestions on how to dress. He and Amelia could hardly wait to show Bridget and Bruno their favorite bar. They stopped for an espresso, of course. The café was large with dark wood and shiny brass to reflect warmth during the long winter days. The town was abuzz with sabot sailboats (eight-foot dinghy sailed by one, and often raced in places around the world) and windsurfers. There was a cycling event bringing hundreds of sports enthusiasts to the old town at the same time they were there. Riva del Garda is also a popular spot for paragliding.

As they strolled around the town the couples chatted. Massimo was excited to speak English, so he and Bruno traded off between the two languages. Massimo was a huge Beatles fan still.

Bridget's Italian was weaker than Amelia's English so they communicated in English. It was easier to get an idea across as they had become more familiar with each other on their second meeting. They shared similar ideas about politics. Because Amelia and Bridget were around the same age, they had seen issues around women's reproductive rights change in both countries. "Ah," sighed Amelia, sadly, "the young women take these things for granted and they can be taken away from them if they are not careful. They forget how hard we fought for them." Bridget agreed, with deep concern. In so many areas, in both countries, it seemed that hard-won progress was at risk.

As sunset colored the sky, the couples parted, each hoping that their friendship would continue with more opportunities for spending time together. Bridget thought she saw a golden eagle drift over the mountain. This was a perfect symbol for their trip coming to an end. Only the long plane ride remained. They were both ready to return to Oregon and Eugene, a place they loved.

Rome

It was a little over a year in late September 2014 when Bridget and Bruno returned to Italy. The couple arrived at the Roma Termini train station thirty-two hours after leaving Eugene, Oregon. On the Leonardo Express, the train that connects the airport to Rome's central train station, they recognized some of the Asian passengers from the plane by the large foam neck pillows that they still wore around their necks. Bridget and Bruno stepped out into the dark evening in a bit of a blur and headed straight for the line of cabs.

They were approached by a cab driver who had never heard of their destination, the neighborhood of Pigneto, but would take them there for 60 euros. The second cab driver said he had heard of their location but then walked off to God knows where, wanting them to follow him to his car. Finally, they noticed a different line of cabs in a brightly lit area and got a licensed cab driver to take them to Pigneto for 20 euros.

Some of their most insightful conversations were with cab drivers. This one spoke Italian and some English. "Things are really down now in Italy. It (the economy) hasn't been this bad since right after the war. Yes, those were gypsy drivers and they are not legal. One day I may have to go without paying for an expensive license, too."

Months before the start of the trip Bridget saw several articles in the travel section of newspapers and magazines about the "most bohemian, newly-renovated section in Rome" for cafés and inexpensive apartments to rent. They would be staying one week in an apartment in Pigneto that she had arranged online through Airbnb.

The driver took them to the address, which was in a dark alley. Bridget and Bruno stood surrounded by their luggage, ringing the doorbell at the gate. Bruno also placed a phone call to their host. After ten nervous minutes (what if nobody showed up, thought Bridget) two men on a scooter stopped beside them.

Si, si, si, si, this was their host Lorenzo and his friend Claudio. These two Romans were just a little younger than Bridget and Bruno. They wore jeans and leather jackets. The lines on their faces suggested some hard living. The apartment was Lorenzo's home. Many of his personal items where there. He was moving into his girlfriend's apartment and Bridget and Bruno would be his last Airbnb guests, because he had found a long-term renter. They learned that he was a professional photographer. His home was artfully decked out with a mixture of family treasures and practical IKEA items. Speaking quickly, he told them dozens of quirky housekeeping details that the weary travelers needed to absorb.

"Don't open this window, don't close that door or it will never open again. Here are the refills for the zappers to plug in to keep the mosquitos away..."

When he took them upstairs, Bridget found herself crawling upwards on all fours. The stairs were narrow and rose higher, step-by-step, than code would allow back home, and one side was completely open to the room below without even a railing to hold on to.

Upstairs there were two bedrooms and a lovely, clean bathroom with a vaulted ceiling accented in rose colored bricks and a Venetian chandelier. Lorenzo, who moved about as if he had drunk three espressos too many, muttered to himself and sprinkled some white powder around the perimeter of the bathroom "because of ants," he said. From then on every step Bridget took in the bathroom was done with a shudder as she wondered what poisons might be in that white powder from the old-looking can.

Lorenzo insisted on taking the weary travelers on a tour of the neighborhood. They trudged down the dark alley with Claudio at the end of the group. Bridget thought that these two were an Italian version of the Marlboro man, only a little more alley-cat.

A friend who was familiar with Pigneto had prepared Bridget for the large African population they encountered. Bridget also noted little places to eat, with signboards advertising prices well below what was typical in the tourist center of the city. There was a youthful population of students and families out in the warm night air, which was thick with humidity. Maybe it would rain soon, Bridget hoped. Lorenzo pointed out places to eat and pick up groceries. He was quick to share his preferences. "I never buy produce or meat from that shop run by the Indians," he said as if to warn them. After they had walked around several blocks they came to a dark street and Lorenzo said, "No need to go there!" Indeed, It did not look inviting.

Men stood around in the unlit street and eyed them as they took a sharp 90 degree turn. "Yes, this is where many of the African illegals live. They won't bother you. The newer groups, the Indians, Middle Easterners and Russians, live further down there." At a pleasant looking trattoria Lorenzo left, saying he would stop by the next day to take some measurements for a repair.

After a satisfying pasta dinner, the weary travelers, full of wine, found their way home. The apartment was not far from the main street of bars where people were still enjoying the late September evening. In fact, the sounds didn't quiet until 4 a.m., by which time Bridget could smell the bread coming out of the oven at the *forno* (bakery) at the end of the alley.

The daylight arrived. They had brought coffee in a sealed package in their luggage but even several cups didn't make Bridget feel less zombie-like. She warned Bruno that she didn't have much vigor as she counted the hours since she'd had a real sleep—nearly three days at this point. Bruno had slept soundly in their new digs. As Bridget showered and dressed, careful not to step in the white powder, she felt weary and, even after showering, hot and sticky. Bruno went out to do a little shopping as she pulled herself up by her bootstraps to begin their first day of adventure.

Bruno had a plan. When he returned, they went to the tobacco shop to purchase bus and subway passes for their week and they got some money from their accounts at the bancomat, then traveled by bus and subway to the area around the American embassy, five-star hotels, and the Borghese gardens. Bruno had read about a small museum with an exhibit of cocktail dresses from the 1950's which he thought Bridget would enjoy.

After walking block after block, and some blocks twice, Bridget insisted they walk into the fancy Westin Hotel and ask the concierge if he knew of this little museum and exhibit. Bruno had written the information on paper. "No," the concierge said as he showed it to his co-worker. Together they stared at it in disbelief. They had never heard of it. He did look the address up and gave them directions, but again they wandered many blocks in vain.

They decided to go to the Borghese Gardens to visit the little café that Bridget remembered. Blocks and blocks later they reached the Cine-Art café on the edge of the gardens. Bridget couldn't sit down soon enough. She ordered a panino, since they hadn't eaten yet and it was 3:00 in the afternoon. The sky was grey and it was humid. Bridget used the substantial paper napkin to blot water from her glass onto her face and neck. Bruno would have loved to have walked the entire garden, but Bridget had hit the wall. Luckily they made it back to Pigneto in time to meet Lorenzo and Claudio as they came to take measurements for the repair.

Bridget and Bruno had a dinner in the neighborhood and planned an early bedtime, since they had an appointment to enter the Vatican Museum at 10:00 am. That would require an early start with buses and subway and grabbing a cappuccino and pastry close to the museum.

Bridget could not sleep. It was hot and sticky. She got up to check on their next Airbnb, in Bari. They had not heard back from their host and needed to know who would meet them and at what time. Turning on the computer, she got into the website for Airbnb and left a message for their host, Vito.

Now, as well as feeling groggy from lack of sleep, she seemed to be developing some allergy symptoms. Lots of sneezing and a stuffy nose made it that much harder to sleep, and in fact she didn't. Bruno once again slept like a log. He was snoring so much that it kept her up, so she tried the bed in the other bedroom.

When Bruno woke up he was ready to take in the fabulous Vatican museum. Knowing Bridget's lack of stamina for large museums, he had studied and mapped the most direct path through. What Bridget only vaguely remembered about the plan was that the last room they would see would be the Sistine Chapel. "Perhaps I should have read the guide books," she thought. Since it was a free day at the museum, saying it was packed was an understatement.

They took in beauty in all forms and manner. The sculpture was grand, the artifacts amazing, the gardens and balconies palatial. There was a room with a modern art collection that she wished she had saved some energy for, and an entire room dedicated to Matisse, one of her favorite artists. On exhibit were designs for the chapel in Vance, France where she and Bruno had once visited.

They shuttled through multiple passageways and Bridget began to feel queasy and claustrophobic. When they entered the crowded Sistine Chapel, she was suddenly hit hard with the need to get into the fresh air. Bruno credited her with the swiftest movement through the Sistine Chapel on record. She did stop in the middle and looked up to see God about to touch Adam's finger, but only for an instant, and then continued as fast as possible to the door and the famous winding stair-case to the exit on the first floor.

The combination of lack of sleep (now four nights), dizziness, unforgiving humidity, and now thirty-six insect bites on her chest had reduced her usual optimistic self to a limp noodle. At a sports bar away from the tourist area, Bruno ordered a Campari spritz. They were the only customers and the wait person said that he wasn't a bartender. That became obvious when he brought a tall glass filled with ice and Campari; three times the amount you would use in a spritz. Bridget's glass of white wine revived her enough to at least get home. Once there she collapsed on the bed and napped. Bruno went out to explore and bring home dinner.

That night they downloaded the first movie on Bruno's laptop. The apartment TV didn't work. This was a very nice escape. Before bed, they tried again to straighten out their reservation in Bari. Bridget was getting really annoyed since their arrival was days away and they couldn't contact their host.

When they awoke, there was still no word from their host in Bari. They got up and put themselves together. It was quite a trick, now, not to step on the white powder in the bathroom, as it had spread a bit further away from the perimeter each day.

They bused to the subway and got off at the Spanish Steps, where they could feel the vibe of the tourists again. There was excitement in the air and people moved faster to arrive at their destinations. The tables outside were full of people of all ages enjoying food and beverages. The pair stopped for a cappuccino and panino before entering the exhibit of Henri Cartier-Bresson's work.

For Bridget, who loved photography, this was one of the high points of the trip. Throughout Cartier-Bresson's career, he had a knack for choosing the decisive moment to take a photo. So many of his photos captured the plight of the downtrodden. He was never spoiled by his success. The extensive exhibit was very moving.

In the same building, a very modern one designed by the American architect Richard Meier which was generally derided by Romans as resembling a mammoth gas station, they saw the Ara Pacis Augustae, the altar of imperial peace to honor the long Pax Augusta. This peaceful spell had allowed Roman civilization to flourish. The altar was built during the emperor Augustus' reign in the first century. Bridget and Bruno were both humbled by this marble wonder. Its very existence raised the question…why not peace?

After several hours of absorbing two extraordinary events, they stopped at a bar for an aperitivo. Next to them sat a husband, wife, and pre-teen from Australia. These were the first tourists they had spoken to since arriving. They were quick to share travel notes. The exchanges in conversation tumbled out of Bridget's mouth. She was so happy to be able to converse in English! They headed home on the subway.

Once again they strolled in Pigneto and had plates of cheese and cured meats and a glass of wine for dinner. They watched as the group of Africans leaning against the building across the street set up their homemade drums for music. Bridget and Bruno stopped in the market run by the pleasant Indian couple for an inexpensive bottle of wine for home and they also stopped in an *enoteca* (a serious wine shop) to get a nice bottle of wine to take to the artist Jack Portland, who they would be visiting by train for lunch in several days. One last stop and each had a one euro shot of grappa. "Now we are truly in Italy," thought Bridget, as she wiped a fresh sheen of perspiration from her forehead and examined the strange bites down her blouse. She was hopeful for sleep this coming night.

On Sunday, while they were returning from their day of touring in the center of Rome, Bruno purchased some cookies from Dolce Maniera, a shop he had found in the guidebook. They climbed down narrow stone stairs to a world famous bakery which did not disappoint. He bought *brutti ma buoni* (ugly but good), small traditional cookies which were something like biscotti. They were sweet, hard, and irregular in form but all the same size. As Bruno reached for his coin purse to pay for the cookies, he realized that he had left it at the neighborhood forno Saturday evening.

The next morning, as they prepared to take the train for a day trip to Fondi, they found that the cookies, which Bruno had left out on a plate in the small kitchen, had been invaded by a colony of ants. It was horrifying! Quickly, they contained them in the trash bag and deposited it in a garbage receptacle before they caught the city bus to Stazione Termini.

Bridget was feeling the heat of the day already and Bruno was glum because he had lost his week-long bus pass as well as euros in his coin purse.

When they went to replace the cookies at the neighborhood bakery on their way to the train station, the cashier had Bruno's coin purse. It was a welcome sight.

On the train to Fondi, Bridget thought about Jack Portland, whom she had met the previous spring at a yard sale in Portland, Oregon. He had been walking with his three-year-old grandson, Max, and pointing to objects and flowers and naming them in Italian. Bridget was captivated by the tender chatter between the nonno and the boy. She quickly summoned her small Italian vocabulary to greet the two. They exchanged stories of their love of Italy as they stood amidst the yard sale items. Bridget rattled off all the places she had visited in her travels with Bruno. Jack Portland said that he had a home in Fondi, just outside of Rome. While they were there in September, why didn't they take the train and join him for lunch?

Bridget was always hearing stories about these sorts of things happening to their friends, Angela and Jerry. They would meet Italians and, before long, they would be staying at their new friends' second home for weeks at a time and become lifelong friends. Bridget jumped at the chance to take Jack up on his offer for lunch. He was from Portland and lived half of the year in Italy. Jack said that he was an artist. Perfect, she thought. Since Bruno was an artist, too, the two men would surely get along.

They exchanged emails before the trip. Jack would meet them at the train station and they would take the bus to his home. As the train pulled into the small station at Fondi, they bounded down the steps and spotted Jack astride a small scooter. After she had introduced Jack and Bruno, Jack suggested that they take the bus and he would ride his scooter beside them, signaling when to get off the bus. Bridget kept her eye on Jack as the bus made a few stops.

Jack signaled them with a hand gesture and they exited the bus. He leaned his small motor bike against the outside of a pocket-sized store, went in, and returned with three pieces of pizza. They were topped, simply, with the reddest, richest, tomato sauce ever. He was proud of his treat. Fondi is known for being a hub of agriculture for Italy. Jack looked at home in Italy, moving with sureness and grace as he wheeled his scooter along the stone road that led to his house.

He told Bruno and Bridget more about the small town of Fondi as they walked past three-story stone buildings. Most of these were residences, with an occasional shop on the ground level. Before the construction of the highway between Rome and Naples in the 1950s, Fondi had been an important settlement on the Roman Via Appia, the main connection from Rome to much of southern Italy.

The ground floor of his home had formerly been a forno. That space was now a utility area with a small bathroom added by the previous owners. The small kitchen, living room and bedroom were on the second floor, with a bedroom and bathroom on the third floor. There was a balcony off the third floor as well. All of the furnishings were purchased with the house from the previous Italian owners. They were large wood pieces; heavy and dark. Bridget wondered how they ever got them up the stairs and into the rooms.

Jack treated them to a light lunch. Everything was fresh: the buffalo mozzarella, the bread, the greens, the salami and other cured meats. They enjoyed the cookies and wine that they brought. The visit was relaxed and satisfying. Over lunch they got to know their new friend. He was a remarkable man, not only for his reputation, especially in Oregon, as an exceptional teacher and artist, but for his gentleness and open demeanor.

They learned that he had purchased his house thirty years ago and lived in it only in the spring and the fall. It did not have heat in winter or a way to cool it in the extremes of summer. The coastal town of Fondi was next to the wealthy resort town of Sperlonga. Jack said that the coastline was the most beautiful he had ever seen. That is something for someone coming from Oregon's beautiful coast to say. Bridget wished they had time to see the coast but they would be catching the last bus of the day to the train. The thought of a beautiful seaside hotel and a departure from Rome sounded refreshing to her.

Jack told them that, five years ago, he had been in the hospital in Fondi for thirteen months. Before traveling to his Italian home he had foolishly drunk some water from a stream in Oregon and a parasite had broken through the wall of his intestine. It caused such a severe infection that several mega rounds of antibiotics were necessary to stabilize him. The huge dose put him in cardiac arrest, and for thirteen minutes he was unresponsive. He had made a slow return to wellness, perfecting his Italian while he was in the hospital.

On this auspicious day they drank to Jack's health. He mentioned the "slow food" movement as something that impressed him. Bridget made a note to look into this when they returned to Oregon. When it was time to leave, Jack walked them to the bus stop to catch their train back to Rome. Bridget asked if she could take a photo as they walked and the two artists, Jack and Bruno, stood side by side for the picture. They were both about the same size and looked very similar; warm, bright-eyes, thinning hair, and a youthfulness that belied their age.

On the train ride home Bridget sneezed frequently. Her nose had started to run again, and she felt the excitement of the day seep away. She did not feel well. Hopefully it was just allergies. As they climbed down the stairs to the entrance to their apartment the thought of a nap became an irresistible idea. But first she checked the computer for messages about their Bari reservation. Still no word from Vito. She would worry about that later.

When Bruno returned from exploring the further sections of the Pigneto, Bridget was just waking up. They went out that evening to a pocket-size bar advertising, on the sandwich board in front, fish platters for four euros. They couldn't pass this up although Bridget couldn't taste much. After a big salad at home they watched *Roman Holiday* starring Audrey Hepburn and Gregory Peck on the laptop before falling to sleep after a memorable day.

They awoke to their last full day in Rome. They were scheduled to travel by train for five hours to Bari the next day, and they still had not heard from their host. Bridget was fuming and exasperated with Airbnb which had been no help trying to solve their dilemma. Bruno and Bridget were in agreement that they needed to make different arrangements for the week. They canceled their pre-paid stay and booked a week in a hotel, Mamma Si Si, in the historic town of Lecce (inland from Bari). This would be their first visit to Puglia, identifiable on a map as the heel of the boot that is Italy. Months later they worked things out with Airbnb and got their refund. It took diligence!

The next morning she awoke feeling hot and sticky. After showering she examined the three dozen bites on her chest, she toweled off, and tried not to step in the white powder that had become a little pasty in the moisture of the bathroom. Bridget put on the same black 100% cotton top that she had worn every day. It had been so humid that only this garment would do. She felt heavy and frumpy as they set off to the bus stop.

For the last bit of sightseeing in Rome, they headed out for the Ponte Rotto (broken bridge) and the Tevere (Tiber). They stopped for a cappuccino and pastry on the way. The buses were exceptionally crowded. They were packed body-to-body into the aisle, and yet when the doors would open, twenty more people would board. On their second bus a group of large women stood in the aisle and would not let them pass. Bruno squeezed through and gestured for Bridget to do the same. She tried twice with no luck. He kept signaling. Finally she barged through with great difficulty.

Bruno had a romantic sounding plan for them to walk on the banks of the Tiber after they had disembarked. If there hadn't been so much garbage and if Bridget had felt better, it might have been fun. Feeling vulnerable in a strange way, she begged him to give up the idea. Her feet hurt. Sweat dripped down her black top. Soon she found out that she had been pick-pocketed while on the bus. Probably someone in the group of women had unzipped her purse and popped up on the bottom of it to cough up her Canon camera. Her spirits sank to such a low point that it took her a little while to rationalize that she still had her iPhone for photos. Also, they hadn't taken her credit card or coin purse. She regretted losing the photo of Bruno and Jack Portland, however.

Near the Tiber they found themselves at the Jewish quarter. They had not been here before and Bridget wasted no time in finding a trattoria for lunch. It was a fancier place than they had been choosing while in Rome, but she insisted on it in the spirit of "living well is the best revenge." Bridget ordered fried squash blossoms with cheese and anchovies and a fried artichoke. Bruno ordered pasta carbonara. They shared tastes and a bottle of white wine. It was a meal that would have made anyone feel better.

The bus rides back to their apartment were even more crowded. Now Bridget felt suspicious of those around her. They were scheduled to go for an aperitivo in the Pigneto with their host, Lorenzo. She decided to beg off and stay behind. When they reached home she began packing, not sad to be leaving Rome this time. She wished they had ridden the hop-on-hop-off bus that circles around the grand monuments in Rome. They did that on their last trip and didn't think they needed to repeat it but she missed it. She stuffed and zipped clothing into her wheeled suitcase, then went downstairs to make a meal of the remaining items in the refrigerator.

Lorenzo, who resembled Anthony Bourdain, the icon of the foodie world, took Bruno to a bar that had been frequented by the filmmaker, Pier Paolo Pasolini, who had lived in Pigneto. This was not the last time Bridget and Bruno's paths would cross with the reputation of Pasolini on this trip. Bridget was happy to hear Bruno's recap of the evening, but did not regret her decision to rest at home.

They ate the leftovers, took a bottle of wine and two glasses upstairs, and watched the TV show *Madam Secretary*.

In the morning they took a cab to the train station.

Lecce

Bridget liked to arrive early before boarding; today she had a little time to observe the general throng of people at Termini Station. The Asian travelers sitting across from them, who were well dressed and surrounded by a significant number of hard-sided suitcases, stood out from the other passengers waiting for trains. She and Bruno watched them chat merrily among themselves. Bridget wondered if they needed so many suitcases for their vacation or possibly they had purchased fashions in Rome? The styles would look lovely on the delicate frames of the sophisticated bunch she watched.

As the train pulled out Bridget said, with some satisfaction, "Arrivederci Roma."

During the five-hour trip to Lecce, Bruno was absorbed in his reading and hardly looked up. Bridget tended her allergy symptoms, tried to sleep, and ended up reading as best as she could through watery eyes. They changed trains in Bari, where they had just enough time to grab an espresso and pastry from the bar in the station before carrying their luggage down the stairs and then up again to platform number five to catch the train further south to inland Puglia, the city of Lecce, capital of its province and also known as the Golden City. Many guide books recommended a visit to this section of Italy which is off the beaten track. From the train window Bridget spotted *trulli* scattered here and there in the countryside. Trulli are one-room circular buildings roughly constructed of stone and built without mortar. She had read that these peculiar-looking Mediterranean dwellings were even sometimes rented to tourists.

From the Lecce train station they took a cab in a circuitous route around the town center, which was largely built in the 16th and 17th century. They arrived at Mamma Si Si's Hotel. The hotel occupied the third floor of a large building just a block off of the town's center and luckily had an elevator. Their room was modern with air conditioning, a TV, a clean bathroom, two leather chairs and a table. A glass door gave them a view of the beautiful Baroque city.

They settled in a bit before exploring the large Piazza Sant'Oronzo, surrounded by buildings on three sides. Lecce is often referred to as the "Florence of the South" because of its beauty. There were interesting places to eat and small upmarket boutiques, antique shops, and bars facing the historic ruins of an amphitheatre and the stone *Sedile* (a former armory) and town hall built in the late 16th century.

Bridget spotted a pharmacy and picked up her walking speed. At the counter she was helped by a young pharmacist. With Bruno's help she described that she had not slept well in a week, had allergy symptoms, and needed something for the mysterious bites on her chest. She discreetly showed the bumps to the young woman. "No, they do not itch," Bridget told her. The pharmacist plucked melatonin, a decongestant, and an antibiotic cream from the shelf and told Bridget that the cost would be sixty-one euros. Bridget was happy to pay for the thought of some relief. Through her head fog, on the way to a gelateria, Bridget realized that she had packed the equivalent to each of these and had them back at their room. Oh well, she thought, feeling a bit dashed, maybe these would be better.

At the gelateria she went for a glass of white wine in lieu of gelato and Bruno selected a savory pastry which they enjoyed standing up at the bar. Visions of the clean bathroom, air conditioning (it was muggy as muggy could be), and bed lured Bridget back to their hotel, where she collapsed. Bruno, as usual, went out to explore and bring back something delicious for dinner.

On his return Bridget was just waking from her nap. Darkness had fallen and rain had come. The city street beyond their window twinkled golden from street lights and lamp light in windows. Bruno had brought wine, vegetables and a meat patty of some sort from a take-out. As they enjoyed the wine from Puglia they watched TV in Italian and then slept well in the cool room.

The next morning, in the hotel breakfast room, they started the day with an ample sweet and savory spread. It included a cappuccino, fruit, juice, yogurt, meats, cheese, crackers and bread. An omelette was an extra charge. The employee, Marco, also checked people in and out of the hotel from the pocket-sized room, no bigger than a closet, adjoining the breakfast room. He was a young man who also studied business at the university in town. Marco spoke English well and was chatty.

Bruno and Bridget learned that Lecce had 30% unemployment for people between 18 and 29. Large land holdings and vineyards were being bought by the Chinese. Many Italians were concerned that the high standards for their traditional wines might be lost. He also informed Bridget and Bruno that the competition for the selection of a 2019

European Cultural Capital was in process, and the officials were judging Lecce that day. To win would help bring more tourism to town.

After breakfast Bruno and Bridget set out for a walk. They thought they might have spotted an official delegation of judges when they visited the Basilica di Santa Croce because, unlike most travelers, the group wore business suits and the women wore heels. Lecce is noted for its own style of ornate architecture, called Barocco Leccese. Bridget liked the fanciful work and had seen similar examples in Noti, Sicily years earlier. Several guide books had referred to the architectural confection carved in sandstone on the front of the building as "the work of hallucinating stonemasons." The exterior was covered with cavorting sheep, dodos, cherubs and beasties. Sadly, some of the work was disintegrating because car fumes and other pollutants were eroding the sandstone.

Inside the basilica Bridget lit candles for the world, her family, and her friend Karen at home, who had asked for an Italian blessing. The outbreak (nearing pandemic) of the Ebola virus in Africa was dominating the news and Bridget's active anxieties. Yet inside the ornate décor of the church everything felt safe and serene.

They left the church and wandered the narrow streets, stopping to look in shops. Bruno had certain things he wanted to show Bridget that he had noted in his independent wanderings. There was a public park that was shady and well kept. They stopped and sat down to eat at an informal restaurant that had salads and panini. They saw many examples of paper mache figures, especially those for a Christmas crèche. Bridget and Bruno were getting better at snapping photos with their iPhones. Since they both had them, it was almost easier than passing the Canon (now history) back and forth.

They went into the upscale store *Society*, which had several locations in Italy. Everything in the store was 100% organic cotton or wool. It was a treat to see quality in bedding and a limited number of garments. There was no room in their luggage or budget for such luxury items but it was fun to see the muted colors that were featured.

Bridget was ready to rest. When they got to their room the internet connection, which had been intermittent, was working at last, so while Bruno continued to explore she spent the next few hours catching up with email and Facebook and was able to post some photos. Everything was fine at home but there was a very disturbing email from Airbnb saying that since they had heard from Vito (not true!) and had not cancelled a week before they were scheduled in Bari, they would not be receiving any refund of the $550 they had prepaid. Bridget could feel the smoke coming out of her ears.

When Bruno came back after his wanderings, it was dusk. She cried in a tearless anguish. Not only did she feel frustrated by their dealings with Vito and Airbnb, she was sick of feeling rotten, and getting bored with her self-imposed exile to the hotel room. She wished she could keep up with Bruno.

Still, she soldiered on. That night they went to see an art installation dedicated to the work of filmmaker Pier Paolo Pasolini at the Castello di Carlo V. Bridget put the black top that she wore every day back on and they walked to the castle entrance and spent the next hour enjoying rooms fit for a king. The exhibit featured photos and relics of the films and the life of Pasolini, who achieved fame as a young author and poet even before entering the film industry.

Some of his films are *Accatone*, *The Gospel According to Saint Matthew*, *Oedipus Rex*, and *The Decameron*. He was murdered in 1975 in still-mysterious circumstances shortly after finishing the anti-fascist film *120 Days of Sodom*. He collaborated with many famous artists including the musical phenomenon from Cleveland, Ohio, Patti Smith. Leaving the castle, Bridget, with sweat dripping down her back, looked with wonder at the sky as they walked home in the airless night.

Dinner at the pizzeria below the hotel was in order. A bottle of good red wine and an antipasto plate big enough to share helped lift her spirits. However, Bridget had to admit that she was not only depressed, but her bites had started to itch. She and Bruno seemed out of tune and out of step with one another. Nothing felt right.

They headed in from the warm, humid night to their cool room and TV. Tomorrow they would take the train early in the morning for a day trip to the coastal town of Otranto.

By 10 a.m. they arrived in Otranto, transported by an ancient, dirty train, in a downpour and with no coast in sight. Bridget and Bruno bought umbrellas and wandered through a quiet, shuttered, residential section. Eventually they saw the bay and restaurants geared to tourists. Bridget couldn't help but sigh in relief. In fact she would have stopped right there but, as usual, Bruno urged her on. They walked along the nearly white seawall to the winding stone streets that led up the steep cliff to the top of the old town. There the Cathederal di Santa Maria Annunziata was perched over the Adriatic.

A wedding was just about to begin outside the large doors of the cathedral. Bridget forgot all of her cares momentarily (well, maybe not the itchy bites) as she and Bruno watched

Italian culture enact one of its most cherished traditions. The bride was helped out of a shiny black car by her proud father, who was decked out in equally formal attire. Her white dress and veil were a mass to deal with. Women in impossibly high heels teetered on the uneven stones. The bride was joined by the young women of the wedding party, who wore long sea green gowns and carried enormous bouquets of white flowers. The mother of the bride hovered and was the first to enter the church on the arm of a young usher. The remaining entourage entered the church along with three young girls who looked about five years old. These girls had flowers in their hair and wore long peach satin dresses.

The church doors remained open for tourists. They had witnessed many wedding parties in their travels, but the opportunity to stand on the sidelines and witness the ceremony was a first. Bridget wondered if this was the parish that the bride's or groom's family had always been part of? It felt that way.

Maybe everyone in such high spirits for this late morning occasion had known these two since they were born. From what she had seen of Otranto's coastal scenery, why would anyone ever want to leave?

The papa solemnly escorted his dark-haired beauty down the long aisle of the church and the groom and his groomsmen looked on in a daze. The high wedding mass followed. Bridget and Bruno stayed for most of it and then slipped around back of the church to the entrance of the 11th century crypt.

Bruno told Bridget about the uneven mosaic floor and its surreal imagery which he had come to see. He was interested in the mosaics and was able to take many photos as Bridget sat on a stone pew and caught her breath. Their early start and the activities of the morning made her feel heavy in her bones.

They left the church and wandered the narrow streets lined with shops featuring folk crafts and beach toys. The recurring item that was typical of the town was a figurine of a round-as-a-beach-ball peasant woman. Almost every shop had her in slightly different sizes and prices.

They had left the hotel in Lecce before having breakfast. As usual, Bridget was ready before Bruno to sit down for a lunch. They wandered down the hill sizing up restaurants and settled on an empty waterfront establishment with several waiters in formal wear standing out front. It wasn't long before the restaurant was totally full. Bridget and Bruno ordered the seafood plate. They were served grilled octopus, sea bass, shrimp, squid, fresh mussels cooked in white wine, and *scapice* (very small fish deep fried in flour and served in bread crumbs and saffron). They split an order of gnocchi and a salad and a bottle of white wine from the region. Everything was exceptionally fresh and tasty. No wonder Otranto was so popular with Italian tourists, thought Bridget.

As they sat and looked out over the blue water all hope was restored for Bridget, who came to Italy to do exactly this. Still, she realized that if all that they did was eat seafood and gaze at the sun and sea, she would be as roly-poly as the folk-art women of Otranto and they would be broke!

Two other wedding parties came into their view, one after the other, followed by their photographers. The sea wall in front of their restaurant was the perfect spot for a photo that would forever mark a most auspicious day.

Bridget and Bruno watched a fisherman run up from the pier below the seawall with a wriggling, live fish in a plastic bag with water in it. He dashed into the restaurant and in just a few minutes came out empty handed and ran back to his perch on the pier for more fishing.

The bride and groom and people from the wedding they had witnessed earlier paraded in front of them on their way to a reception somewhere close, it would seem, since they were all on foot, or in the women's case, on their stiletto heels.

The meal and the moment were outstanding. The sun had come out and there was a gentle breeze coming off the water. This had a stunning effect on all of the wedding veils. The brides moved like exotic white birds, laughing and posing with their grooms.

Bruno wanted to explore the castle built by the Aragonese (1485-98) at the center of the town. Otranto now was a mere shadow of what it once was—one of Rome's main ports for trade with Asia Minor and Greece. Bruno headed off at a brisk pace. Bridget opted to sit just outside of the restaurant on a low stone wall and wait. They still had the hike back to the train station and then from the train station in Lecce back to their hotel. No worries of enough exercise with Bruno around!

What a spectacular day, she thought. She wondered what her life would be like in the future since she had promised Bruno that she would make no more plans for trips to Italy until he was ready. She had pushed for this trip (maybe even the last five) without first getting Bruno completely onboard.

Once they were in Italy, Bruno always enjoyed himself immensely and with gusto. The problem was it was nearly impossible to pull him away from his glass work. Bridget knew that their travels inspired his work. When they were home he burrowed himself deeply in stained glass residential and public projects, language studies, and learning computer code for web design.

Bridget's interests were less tangible and mostly about supporting her home or family. Since her retirement from over thirty years in early childhood education she felt she had had enough of a career! She gardened, shopped, cooked, helped with her granddaughter, planned family events, lit candles, and once a month worked with a group from her church to provide a nourishing breakfast for three-hundred homeless people.

Bruno and Bridget were very different people. Bruno had an intellect which he could wrap around any subject. Bridget was intuitive and emotionally intelligent. She had little interest in detailed information and would rather follow the emotion of a storyline. They had made their relationship work for twenty years. Looking forward to a next trip to Italy had been a high point for Bridget. It was her passion in her well-ordered life. Bruno experienced it as an interruption to his time in his studio. Once in Italy, Bridget had a hard time keeping up with him!

That evening, upon returning to Lecce, they ate a light meal and had a glass of wine before tucking in for the night. Bridget took a long shower and enjoyed the fluffy towels in their hotel room. She fell asleep as a coolness had finally come to the town.

They had one more day in Lecce. It was Sunday, and they awoke to another hearty hotel breakfast. They wandered through the ancient center of town and through a more ordinary business section toward the large cemetery. On their way they passed a group of men decked out in vintage sports attire standing beside antique bicycles. A dozen smiling fellows in caps, goggles, herringbone, tweed or linen jackets, knickers with knee socks, vintage shoes and gloves stood beside bikes from the last century. The centerpiece was a two-wheeler with a gelato concession neatly fitted between the handle bars. It looked like it had seen many a happy customer! Bruno and Bridget took photographs but none of their snaps managed to capture the uniqueness of the encounter.

They walked for twenty more minutes and within a huge park they arrived at the cemetery that was the resting place for the town's previous generations. There were modest grave markers, elaborate stone markers, and mausoleums for generations of relatives. Half the population of Lecce was visiting too. Relatives were grooming the graves, adding flowers, and paying respect to the departed. Presumably, next they would go to Mamma's for the Sunday dinner. This was a part of Italian tradition that Bruno and Bridget had not witnessed before. The two walked somberly around the statuary and cars.

Bridget thought of her parents who had passed away within months of each other fourteen years previously. The small inheritance they had left her made it possible for her to retire and travel. Bruno walked by her side solemnly. Neither spoke.

On their return to town, the retro bicycle gang was gone. Many places were closed on Sunday. They took a quick look at a small exhibit of photos of the Touring Club Italiano that were on display in a public building in the center of the old town. Founded in 1894, the group takes credit for "inventing" tourism for Italians. The collection of black and white photos showed groups of Italians (always well dressed) all over the globe enjoying the world by car, train, and plane.

For their last meal in Puglia, they chose a modern-looking restaurant specializing in seafood, near the hotel. The fresh fish was on ice. You ordered it by the *etto* (Italian measurement that equals 100 grams to 1 etto) and they cooked it for you. It was a bit pricey, and yet a wonderful experience, since the wait staff brought them vegetables and a dessert on the house. The restaurant would likely be closed on Monday so this late afternoon meal would end their week. Bruno and Bridget were the last customers and watched as the staff cleaned up, probably anxious to get home to their family meal. This was a rare non-traditional regional eatery. It appeared to be a huge success, and offered a nice variation on classic cuisine.

Bruno and Bridget lingered at the historic center, holding hands as the light faded and the golden lights came on. Then they returned to their hotel to pack and finish the bottle of wine they had saved. Bridget set the box of tissues next to her as they settled in to watch the soap opera *Tempesta D'Amore*. Since their first trip to Italy fifteen years earlier, they had made a point of watching this show every time they could. They were always able to pick up where they had left off, Bridget thought, as she lay back and scratched the bites and applied the antibiotic.

Matera

Bridget didn't realize it, but when they boarded the train she was headed to her most strange and memorable adventure, one not entirely pleasant. This train ran on a different line than the familiar Trenitalia, and she and Bruno traveled comfortably for an hour in a modern glass-sided cube that looked like something from Disney World. These small modern cars had been added just a year ago. Bruno was uncertain about which was their stop. Luckily they decided to step off the train with all of their luggage at its first stop, where they learned very quickly through some rapid conversations with travelers on the platform that only the lead car would be going to the UNESCO World Heritage Site of Matera. They ran to the lead car and jumped in just moments before it left the station. Bruno let out a rare sigh of relief for the deliverance from "what might have been." Bridget wiped the sweat from her eyes and face and she hoisted her luggage up on the overhead rack once again.

As of October 2014 few tourists outside of Italy had yet discovered Matera, the capital of its province in the region of Basilicata. Using a boot as a metaphor for the outline of Italy, Matera is slightly inland, at the arch of the high-heeled boot. Bridget had read about Matera's extensive series of *sassi* (Paleolithic caves) later inhabited by Benedictine monks. The town also had *caveosi* (man-made rock dwellings). From a distance Matera looked like it had been carved out of a single huge piece of stone.

Because of its resemblance to Jerusalem, Matera has been used as a set for biblical films. Mel Gibson's *The Passion of Christ* and Pier Paolo Pasolini's *The Gospel According to Saint Matthew* had both been filmed there. The filming of *Ben Hur* with Morgan Freeman would begin the month after their visit.

The couple would be staying in a caveoso on one of Matera's ancient streets. The building dated back to 1500, when their bed and breakfast had been a monastery and, later, a convent.

When they got off the train Bruno pulled out the instructions from their hosts and read them aloud: "not far from the train." Bridget had learned by now that that meant a long haul. These transitions in their travels always put Bridget in a bad mood. She lowered her head and felt the sweat run in rivulets down her back and front. She pulled her forty pounds of luggage over the rough streets a few paces behind Bruno, who was always upbeat about how close the unknown destination would be.

They trudged on through a business district typical to a small Italian town. At its edge, the ancient cave dwellings began. There was a stark difference as the landscape became steep and was solid rock with hardly any vegetation. Rock beneath their feet, rock walls of the caves on one side and then the other. They twisted and turned around and down flights of ancient stone steps. Bruno would round a curve and be completely out of Bridget's sight. They saw no other people as they traveled on. It seemed they had entered another world. Every cave they passed was empty.

Up ahead Bridget saw three tables set up outside a doorway, with tablecloths, wine glasses and table settings. A young woman wandered out of the tiny restaurant, and Bridget thought about how welcome it would be to stop and get their bearings, have lunch, and drink a glass of wine. But she knew that Bruno would not go for that idea, so she continued onward. It was useless to suggest anything until they had located their destination. With a sinking feeling, Bridget realized that Bruno did not have a hell of an idea of where they were heading.

They wandered five minutes more, which felt like fifteen to Bridget. She had to go to the bathroom badly and couldn't get that nice restaurant out of her mind. Bruno looked back to see her face screwed up and her spirit balking. She required a kiss. They decided that she would stand where she was and he would go ahead to scout their location.

There were no street signs, no ninety-degree corners, no numbers on the doors. Bridget watched Bruno disappear around the bend and worried, "I might never see him again." The fear seemed to become a reality. She stood there in tears, with no trace of her usual resourcefulness. She had hit a wall. Unable to find her way forward or backward on the descending circumference of Matera, she could only wait for Bruno to return. Never had she felt that she was in such a godforsaken spot. The October early afternoon heat and humidity engulfed her. Nothing in the landscape was remotely familiar. Her bites began to itch as the perspiration gathered on her chest.

She tried to calm her mind by thinking of a song. Her usual go-to, the Shaker tune, *'Tis a Gift to Be Simple*, fell from her mind to the pit of her stomach fast. A few years ago when she, Bruno and three friends were stuck in an elevator for an hour in Assisi on Easter afternoon, waiting for someone to drive in from the country to fix the elevator, she could think of all kinds of songs to sing. Everyone in the elevator sang *John Jacob Jingleheimer Schmidt* to pass the time.

Bridget stood frozen and afraid. Finally, Bruno reappeared with good news. He had reached their hosts on his telephone. The weary travelers retraced their steps and returned to the same restaurant they had passed. Their B&B hostess, Donata, was waiting there to walk them to her bed and breakfast.

Donata, who was half the size of Bridget, sized up her new boarder. From her expression, Bridget surmised that Donata saw her as a traveler on the verge of a breakdown. Quickly she took over Bridget's luggage, and with light feet and an annoying amount of ease, aimed them in a new direction. They passed some caves that had been modernized and were inhabited. They had tall Italian-style windows, doors and balconies. They passed a café. When they stopped they were in front of a door in the rock wall. It looked like it would lead to a garage. Once inside, they learned that their room had been a food storeroom for the monastery. It was handsomely crafted of stone with arches. The IKEA kitchen was not equipped; it was closed for the fall since there would be fewer tourist bookings. Donata would prepare their breakfast in the big adjoining house.

Their hostess oriented them to their new digs and had them fill out the necessary paper work. They would be staying for two nights. The wi-fi worked sometimes. The humidifier might need emptying during their stay. The bathroom was clean. The small shower enclosure had been partially repaired with duct tape. Bridget knew that the tiny Italian shower contraptions were flimsy, even when in good order, but she didn't think the slapdash repair would be a problem.

As soon as Donata left them alone a tremendous downpour began. They could hear the rain beat sideways on the front of their building. The temperature cooled, even inside. They listened to the crackling of thunder, relieved that they had made it to the shelter of their stone dwelling.

They settled in and, by some miracle, Bridget was able to make two calls on WhatsApp (a telephone app that allows international calls at no charge if the receiver also uses the app). First she called her daughter Sarina in Portland, Oregon. Things were fine there. Then she talked to her son, Jaan, in Charlottesville, Virginia. Nothing could have been more of a tonic than talking to her children, however briefly.

After the rain slowed, Bruno and Bridget felt settled-in enough to poke around their neighborhood for a restaurant. Bridget soon spotted a bar and Bruno wisely let her lead them in. It had been that kind of a day.

They ordered panini and wine and were content to watch a few workers come in and order food and drink at the end of their day. There was a small piece of fabric hanging from the ceiling, slightly bigger than a placemat, that had some words about Matera on it. They would eventually see many more of these, including one they hadn't noticed on the large house adjacent to their B&B. Bruno asked in Italian what they were for, and learned that Matera (like Lecce) was contending to be a 2019 European Cultural Capital. Days later they cheered when they heard Matera was announced one of the winners, chosen over well-known places like Siena and Florence.

On Bridget and Bruno's return to their apartment they got a better view of the ancient city winding below and above them. Bridget estimated that the climb both ways was at about a 70 degree angle. "Not today," she thought. They had bread and cheese from their luggage as a snack before turning into bed with their reading.

The next morning Donata served them breakfast upstairs in the big house. Bridget peeked into the extra-large modern kitchen and the formal, chic living room off in another direction. Their hostess did not offer a tour. Donata had run out to the bakery minutes before to get fresh pastries, which she served with yogurt, cheese, fruit and coffee. Like all the middle-aged Italian women Bruno chatted with, Donata was soon in the palm of his hand. His attention to detail and his knowledge of the fine qualities of the Italian language and culture made him very popular. Luckily, thought Bridget, Donata soon had to run off to her job.

They began their trek up and down the sassi, not encountering many other people as they traveled. Several of the rock walks opened onto large flat piazzas that held a handful of small businesses or a church. They noticed the white flags everywhere, and soon they saw what looked like a delegation of judges absorbed in writing on their clipboards and looking the buildings up and down.

Bridget and Bruno located a tourist area where, for five euros, they could enter a cave dwelling outfitted like it would have been in the past. The line was not long. They entered the two rooms where a family—perhaps two parents, four children, and a donkey—might have lived as recently as 1900. There was a full-sized paper mache donkey happily tethered by the fireplace. The cart that the donkey would have pulled was also tucked inside, next to the bed. Beside the bed was a blanket on a mound of hay where the oldest child would have slept. One drawer of a large chest was pulled out, and their guide said the next child slept there. Another child slept on top of the chest, and the baby would sleep in bed with the parents. High on an indentation in the rock surface was the family accordion. Grain was kept in another chest, and a large loom was tucked away where the ceiling sloped down to the wall. A hole in the wall was packed with ice to keep things cool. The rustic kitchen included a cage for the hen. It was cleverly laid out and luckily they were spared the smell which, when all added up, could have been a knockout.

As they wandered outside Bridget was relaxed enough to joke with Bruno and take some cheesy selfies with the town as a backdrop. She had gone from resistance to disbelief to serious respect for Matera. They looked out from a waist-high rock wall built above a steep 200-foot drop and watched small groups of tourists arrive in buses.

Settling on a late lunch in a tiny restaurant similar to the one they had first encountered, Bridget had ravioli in pumpkin sauce with truffle oil. Bruno had pasta with truffle sauce. Everything was as flavorful as if they were in Rome or Florence at a fancy restaurant. The couple next to them was also from the U.S. They were attractive and friendly and, as they ate their lunch, the travelers chatted.

They were around the same age as Bridget and Bruno. The woman revealed that she had planned this adventure, adding that all her husband wanted to do when they traveled was go to Paris, look in bookstores, and sit in cafés. She was so done with Paris. Bridget wondered to herself how it was going for them here? The husband looked sullen.

They returned to their apartment. Bruno would explore a bit more before a light snack and preparations for an early start the next day. Before falling asleep, Bruno emptied the dehumidifier for the third time in less than two days. In the 1950s, the impoverished inhabitants of the caves were forced to leave their homes. Humidity, mold, no electricity or running water, plus living with the animals made the caves incubators for cholera and other diseases. The adult life expectancy at that time was 35, and the infant mortality rate was 50%. In the 1970's artists and adventurers repopulated the caves. To make them less hazardous they installed modern conveniences.

The next day, Bruno and Bridget had plans to call a taxi after breakfast. There were a few street spurs where a taxi could pull in. The notion that a taxi could come close to their B&B and take them to the bus stop delighted Bridget. Before leaving Oregon she had announced to Bruno that she wanted to use taxis more on this trip. Bridget remembered some of their previous difficult transitions between train to lodging on foot. Bruno took these as a badge of honor. Not Bridget. They also had intended to rent a car some time in their travels, but so far had made do without one.

Their taxi dropped them off and they stood waiting for the bus. Bridget blotted the moisture that was forming on her forehead and chest in the sun. Her bites were beginning to itch. She and Bruno weren't 100% sure they were in the right spot. Nothing said "bus stop," and where they stood looked like a random open lot. But eventually the bus appeared. They boarded and began the five-hour journey west to Naples.

Naples

Bridget settled her two pieces of luggage and herself on the bus. She and Bruno both felt tentative about the five-hour ride with no bathroom stop, but their worries were soon forgotten as they relaxed into the seats of the Pullman-style bus that was traversing inland across the "ankle" of the boot to the west coast and Naples.

On her phone, Bridget caught up with news of the spreading Ebola pandemic. Each report of this uncontained, often deadly, virus brought her chills. Bruno assured her that even though they were close to Africa, the chance of someone who was contagious getting to Italy was not very likely. This defied logic, to Bridget, but it turned out to be true. Even though cases of the disease came into the United States through doctors, nurses and aid workers, there were none yet in Italy.

Bridget focused on some mindful breathing. Eyes closed, breath from the abdomen, in slowly, then push out even more air than was taken in. She never slept well before a travel day, and the previous night had been no exception. Years before, she vowed never to visit southern Italy. There was a fear related to her childhood. Growing up in Youngstown, Ohio, mafia-related car bombings were a trademark of the city's gritty history. "Not around where we lived," her sister Anna had recently reminded her when they were talking before the trip.

Yet in spite of her vow, four years earlier Bridget had traveled to Sicily with Bruno and now they were in the south again. The week spent in Ortygia, Sicily, on the Mediterranean was one of her fondest memories. So she was game to try Naples. The recent warnings from Naples were about dodging the traffic, nothing more. She watched the flat brown landscape from the window, applied ointment to her bites, and tried to remain cool and calm.

As the sun was dimming to dusk, they arrived at the train station and bus terminals, a huge industrial-looking complex. Before Bruno could bat an eye, Bridget had hailed a cab. The driver pointed out the castle on the bay as he drove them through the city. He warned about certain sections to avoid. He parked the cab in the middle of a shopping area with an outdoor café, pointing to the address on the side of a gigantic door. They stood with their luggage facing the door as Bruno made contact with their Airbnb host Marco, who appeared quickly and showed them into the building to their apartment on the fifth floor. Luckily, there was an elevator (coin operated).

The apartment was just as it had been described and photographed online. Everything was in order: the air conditioning worked, as did the washer, TV (with several English speaking channels), stove, fridge, CD player, and fan. After Marco left, Bruno and Bridget went to the Grand Bar, downstairs and immediately outside their door, and ordered a spritz aperitivo. This was delivered with enough snacks and finger food to tide them over until they could get some groceries.

As they sat in the warm October evening sipping their drinks, smiles crept over their faces. So far, so good, thought Bridget. Around them groups of young men in smart Italian suits were ending the day with a drink. The atmosphere was charged with good spirits. Two young mothers, also dressed to the nines, with infants in carriages and shopping purchases stuffed where they could, were doing the same thing. Several couples out for the evening chatted and smiled at each other in that knowing way, much as Bruno and Bridget did.

In the morning, after a very restful sleep and enough coffee to fuel them, Bruno led the way on their first exploration of Naples. Their apartment was in a posh shopping area—Fendi, Ferragamo, Dolce & Gabbana, Dior, Cartier, and Tiffany were just a few of the small stores in their neighborhood. The displays changed almost daily, making it a pleasure to window shop.

To get to the funicular they had to cross several busy streets. This was like an extreme sport, Bridget thought. They hoped that the car would stop when they established eye contact with the driver and stepped into the crosswalk. They had been warned that this was essential to avoid being run over. Each crossing felt like a very close call to Bridget.

At the funicular, they relaxed once onboard the tiny car (one of twenty), which was on a track that ascended steeply inside a tunnel-like windowless building. When they exited, they discovered they were in a tree-lined boulevard of shops and cafés. This was the Vomero neighborhood. Theirs, below, was Chiara. Vomero was home to the stores where the locals shopped.

Bruno consulted his map and they wandered further to the entrance of an estate that had been turned into a park.

Bridget wondered how he knew that at the end of the half-mile trail there would be a small villa with a garden that was perfectly perched to overlook the Bay of Naples. Bruno was full of sweet surprises. The scene was breathtaking, even with a slight haze in the air. Far below, the water sparkled in the bay in the late morning sun.

The couple traveled back through the area of small shops and onto one of four funiculars to the bay below. It seemed like the perfect moment for pizza, done in the way of the napolitani. The spot they chose, with outdoor seating under umbrellas, turned out to be very famous. Photos of New York City mayor Bill De Blasio photographed at the very same restaurant were visible from every table.

The table of young boys and girls to their left was lively with chatter. The girls were thin and elegantly dressed even for their age and the boys were healthy and fresh looking too. Their pizzas took up all of the space on the large plates in front of them. The young women ate only the center of the round pizza, avoiding the outer crust. When Bruno and Bridget's classic Margarita pizza arrived, they decided it earned its claim to fame. Nothing was left on their plates at the end! The tomato sauce and simple mozzarella cheese, including the paper-thin, brick-oven roasted crust, was unforgettable.

The day was warming up and the pavement was radiating heat as they walked back to their apartment. Bridget did a load of laundry, hanging items on coat hangers and putting them in the small closet where the heat exchanger was throwing off heat. Then she napped while Bruno went out to explore. More frightful coverage of the Ebola outbreak dominated the news. The air conditioning kicked in and the late afternoon was comfortable inside.

The next day they started early enough to visit three churches before lunch. One was the Chapel Sansevero where they stood in line to view the famous sculpture, The Veiled Christ by Guiseppe Sanmartino (1753). It is the body of the dead Christ covered by a transparent shroud of the same marble. Bridget admired it as her stomach started to grumble.

They were near the old market of Naples which now sold trinkets, cheap imported plastic household items, and had an occasional cheese or wine store. They had lunch in an unlikely place that ended up being one of their best and most reasonable meals. They took their time sharing some pasta plates, finishing with coffee and grappa. The regulars came in for the cooking at the restaurant called Mamma's.

On their way home they stopped in a church. When they came out Bridget smiled brightly and lingered by an accordion player, maybe a moment too long. When she and Bruno turned to leave, the accordion player followed them. They ducked around corners and picked up their pace to a run. Bridget broke away from Bruno and entered a fancy bridal shop. Five minutes later, when she poked her head out, Bruno smiled and said the coast was clear. As they walked home Bridget chuckled to herself at the thought of her first ardent Italian pursuer in all her nine trips to Italy.

The rest of their week in Naples continued like this, up early and out before the heat and humidity of the October afternoons became too much for Bridget. She was happy to retire to the apartment and read or watch TV until Bruno returned and they would have a quiet evening, snacking at home and watching TV.

Bridget never dreamed October in Naples would feel so uncomfortable. She asked several people if this was unusual weather and everyone said that it was typical.

Evidently she had been off in her calculations of what a perfect time for travel would be.

One lunch time, when she and Bruno exited the funicular at the top of the town, they stopped at a small food stall for fried squash blossoms, calamari, and shrimp and potatoes piled in a paper cone. The young man who served them spoke English and suggested that Naples was a lot like San Francisco. Bridget immediately saw the similarities. Both were vertical cities on a bay with a feminine feel. The server said that he had worked in a pizzeria in San Francisco and he believed that the people of Naples were characters with big personalities, like those creative folks in San Francisco. That resonated with her, too.

In the portraits in the museum they visited, Galleria di Palazzo Zevallos Stigliano, she saw, through the centuries of portraits, a softness and sweetness in the faces of the Neapolitans. The same was evident in the people they encountered on the streets and in the piazzas, evidenced by a soft gleam in their eye, the lightness of their step, the cock of their hat.

On the streets, recent efforts to increase recycling were paying off. The city was clean; garbage was picked up. The people were upbeat.

Bridget and Bruno could walk most places and managed to visit two of Naples' five castles. They toured the opera house during the day and, in the evening, Bruno went back to one of the oldest opera house in Europe to see Donizetti's *L'Elisir d'Amore, The Elixir of Love.* Bridget chose not to go because it started late, it was still hot, she didn't have formal clothes and Bruno would insist on walking because "it wasn't too far away."

Their big outing was by hydrofoil boat to the island of Procida. That was heaven for Bridget. *The Bicycle Thief* and

The Talented Mr. Ripley both had scenes that were filmed there, and the island was perfect by any measure. Boats of all sizes were docked around the circumference of the island. Several churches and the government buildings were at the top of the town. They witnessed a number of wedding parties outside of churches. In one, the groom was getting into a red Ferrari which was to be the "get away" car. Bridget was twenty-five feet away from the groom. She couldn't help but notice the Playboy bunny tattoo in the flesh behind his ear.

A small shuttle bus took Bridget and Bruno to the Lido of Procida. Watching a handful of Italian bathers swim in the ocean was a new experience for them. The beaches were not crowded in the hot October sun. They sat outside a restaurant under a large awning, enjoying a glass of cold white wine, and watched three pensioners swim for twenty five yards, back and forth, in the calm sea. Bridget thought she would like to be in the water with them. Later, Bridget and Bruno shared a panino as they sat on a dock near the slips for the yachts that bobbed further out in the water.

As she looked at the beautiful island scene with contentment and homesickness, she felt the bittersweetness of this moment. She missed her family in Oregon and Virginia. She missed their condo in the high-rise with its bathtub. It happened on every trip— three weeks out, Bridget had a case of the traveler's blues. She recognized this pattern and looked at Bruno. He was smiling to himself. At three weeks Bruno was relaxed and had finally left the cares of his work life behind.

She and Bruno headed back to the hydrofoil. They would head by train to Tuscany two days later.

Montepulciano

Bridget had first said the word, Montepulciano, in connection with a red table wine that she and Bruno would purchase occasionally when they first met twenty years ago. Bruno, who knew about Italian wine, had told her, "I'm usually not disappointed when I choose a wine with Montepulciano somewhere on the label." The full-mouthed sound of the word became linked in her mind to a rich and lovely Italian place. Now, many years and bottles of Italian wine later, they were heading to the hill town Montepulciano.

The train from Naples moved north into Tuscany. The landscape became one of picture-perfect contours of rolling hills, iconic stands of tall, cylindrical cypress trees, vineyards, villages, and hairpin turns around hills and more hills.

Bridget and Bruno would be in Montepulciano for five days. Their friends Angela and Jerry had recently stayed just outside the city. Angela stressed that you needed a car, which Bruno and Bridget would not have. The expense and bother seemed unnecessary. Bruno was convinced he would be able to use some form of public transportation. However, buses ran infrequently, the bus station was on the edge of town and they weren't yet aware of the shuttle into the center. Bridget wished for an easy way to get to traverse the town in the annoying humidity.

Over the phone, Bruno and their landlady Cinzia sorted out how to get from the train station to their apartment. She eventually found them wandering with their luggage and drove them to their rental. Bruno and Bridget would be staying in the former grain storehouse, now an Airbnb decked out with IKEA furnishings in the kitchen and bath. Their rental had a modest table with chairs and bed. Cinzia lived above in the five-hundred-year-old stone dwelling. She was a perky, dark-haired beauty and single. Bruno was the one who talked with her in his well-practiced Italian. Bridget made a note to herself to resume her Italian studies upon their return to Oregon.

After they settled in, they set out to explore, pick up a few groceries, and find the closest spot in town where they could pick up wi-fi. But first they sat at the wooden table outside a café and had a memorable glass of wine as they caught up on several days' messages on their devices. Hmmmm. Bridget noted that the wine was decidedly good. It was served in a large-globed glass. The flavors and essence of the wine were heady. They would return many times to this spot because it had, in the end, the best free wi-fi reception in Montepulciano.

The light was dimming in the hill town. The little shops with high-end goods, some handcrafted, were taking in their sandwich boards. Families with small children strolled by on their way home or to buy gelato. Tourists could be seen and heard (a few loud American voices grated on the quiet surroundings) returning from the wine tours at nearby vineyards. The sound of china and glassware being set out for the evening clinked in the background.

Bridget and Bruno found a small grocery store at the bottom of the hill. This one did not cater to tourists. The owner lovingly sliced them meat and found a complementary cheese in the covered case. They chose some local wine at a reasonable price, then wearily wandered up hill to their windowless, somewhat damp, home away from home. Bridget noticed that her clothing felt slightly moist because of the humidity in the room. After plates of the local fare, they settled under the bedding to snuggle and watch Italian TV before dozing off for the night.

They were up bright and early the next morning. Bridget dressed and went outside to test the temperature and locked herself out of the apartment while Bruno was in the shower. Still, she was grateful that she at least had clothes on as she stood awkwardly waiting. She knocked and called Bruno's name in a big voice but there was no response. She surveyed her surroundings. Only large stone buildings with no help in sight. The ten minutes seemed like an hour until Bruno was done with his shower and dressing and could hear her outside.

They climbed to the top of the town, to the Cathedral of Santa Maria Assunta, built between 1594–1680. Bridget lit candles in the pale morning light. Bruno studied the cathedral's features, especially the mosaics and the terra cotta altar by Andrea Della Robbia.

Outside in the piazza, adjacent to the Palazzo Comunale which was fashioned after Firenze's Palazzo della Signoria, Bridget and Bruno waited for the town shuttle bus (there was one after all). At the bottom of the town was the bus station, a sterile post-war building where many locals hung out and played cards. Bruno made arrangements for their future travel day trip to Passignano, where they would meet their old friend Mara.

Their next stop was market day. They found lines of food carts and many stalls selling domestic wares (can openers, toilet tissue, shower caps). There were sweaters and clothing needed by the locals. Bridget and Bruno purchased fried fish and vegetables and sat and watched many uplifting exchanges as they ate. Bruno got up and returned with a paper cup of red wine for them to share. They had planned to stop at the porchetta truck, as they had vowed early in their Italian travels never to pass one up, but the rare chance to have fried seafood trumped even the simple, fresh cut pork sandwich.

On the way home they purchased beans in a can, tomatoes, cured meats, garlic, hard cheese, and bread. Next they stopped in one of the dozen storefronts where it is possible to taste and order wine from the local vineyards and chose two bottles based on their tasting. Once again Bridget reasoned that this wine from Montepulciano (and there were dozens) might be her favorite wine. It was dry, balanced, spicy and typical of the Sangiovese blends. They chose the younger rosso that was more affordable than the Nobile di Montepulciano. It is not to be confused with Montepulciano d'Abruzzo, which is from another region in the south and also very good. They also stopped at the high-end Tuscan linen shop. Bridget purchased several tea towels that would be handy as gifts.

That night, in their flat, she copied the following from a Lonely Planet article about Montepulciano: "Exploring this reclaimed narrow ridge of volcanic rock will push your quadriceps to the failure point. When this happens, self-medicate with a generous pour of the highly reputed Vino Nobile while drinking in the spectacular views over the Val di Chiana and Val d'Orcia." Indeed, she thought.

Bridget looked forward to seeing Mara the next day. The last time Bridget and Bruno had seen Mara was a year and a half previously when they had spent nearly a month living next door to her in Assisi.

Mara had always been unusual. Growing up in rural Pennsylvania, she developed a passion for Italian opera that she shared with her father. She spent her high school years humming arias and writing down librettos. As a grown woman she developed her own style of dress. She would often wear a knit head covering with an opening for the face and another hat on top of that. She was medium to small build and since she had come to Italy she had thrown off her knee and back braces and no longer had joint pain. She had required them in Eugene and took them to Italy and attributed her cure to all the climbing she did in the hills of her adopted hometown.

Mara had short brown hair and lively blue eyes. Her hands, though small, were the hands of a baker, which Mara had been for many years with notable success. Bridget had met Mara in the early 80s and they clicked. Mara had given her great advice about men and life in general. Bridget might have given up hope of finding a mate if Mara, who had a twenty year career as a marriage and family counselor, hadn't convinced her to keep her heart open. Soon after, Bridget met Bruno. Mara was a famously good cook, too. When Jaan, Bridget's son, was fourteen, he swooned when they all shared a camping trip and Mara performed miracles with food over the campfire, proving that "the way to a man's heart is through his stomach." Bruno met Mara not long after he met Bridget, twenty years previously. He enjoyed Mara's friendship and they shared a love of Italy. Bridget was pleased that Bruno also cherished her eccentric friend.

In fact, Mara had introduced them to Italian culture on Bridget's first trip to Italy with Bruno, marching them immediately upon their arrival to the Mercato Centrale in Florence for boiled beef panini. Never mind visual art or visiting churches, Italy was all about food for Mara.

On some of these adventures Luigi, Mara's ex-husband and still fast friend, was with them. The four of them had spent time together in Florence, in Bologna, in Gubbio, and in Spoleto. Then there was the trip that Mara simply remained permanently in Assisi instead of returning to Eugene and has been there ever since (which in part explains why Luigi is an ex-husband). She and Luigi remained the closest of friends. Bridget adored Luigi and felt he was someone she could also depend on. With diligence, Mara managed to obtain her *permesso* (an official document that enables ex-patriots to stay in Italy permanently and to receive health benefits). After careers as a cook, a baker, and a therapist, Mara became a gattara.

A gattara is a woman who feeds and cares for cats, both the strays and the opportunists. She rises every morning at 5 a.m. to join forces with the other cat women, the gattare. Working alone or in pairs the women travel from the top of Assisi to the bottom, often performing first aid or getting a cat to the vet if necessary. Occasionally a male friend, a gattaro, joins them. They raise money through a cat organization to have wild cats spayed or neutered. Through every kind of weather, Mara joyfully ministers to her four-pawed friends.

Leaving Montepulciano, Bridget and Bruno made their way to Lago Trasimeno and the lakeside town Passignano where they would meet Mara. They had met in this same way six years earlier. It was an easy bus and train connection through farm country for Mara (from Assisi) to Italy's fourth-largest lake.

As soon as Bridget and Bruno got off the train they found a bench where they could wait for Mara to arrive.

Bridget's heart rose to her throat as she watched Mara step down from the train. What a sight for sore eyes, she thought, as Mara trudged toward them, bundled up in spite of the mild day and wearing a backpack with provisions and items like extra shoes and sweaters in case the need would arise in the next four hours. Mara looked good. Bridget believed she was aging backwards. Mara would agree and say it was from all of the olive oil, cheese, salami and wine. She looked a bit like Helen Mirren if Helen were playing the role of a pensioner and gattara.

The three friends embraced, kissing two cheeks all around. They made their way through the small tourist town to the lake. Mara seemed distracted by her tale of Cleopatra's (yes, they remembered Cleopatra) feline revolution in the neighborhood. Mara had nearly missed the bus to the train because she had to wrest command from the black temptress to allow the other cats to get to the food outside Mara's gate. The cat tales continued as they walked through a pleasant neighborhood with fenced courtyards, geraniums and inviting doorways. Mara stopped in her tracks in great surprise to announce, "Why don't I come here more often? I love it here!" By then they were near the lake and could hear it gently lapping the shore. Small boats and pedal water floats dotted the edge. "And Rosito…", Mara continued, filling Bruno and Bridget in with the latest news of her most favorite cat of all.

They found their special restaurant, which was empty, but the owner was happy to serve them lunch. Bruno gave Mara the rechargeable batteries that would work in

Mara's charger, and Bridget presented the plastic lids for cat food cans that Mara had also requested. She always had a wish list for things she simply couldn't find in Assisi and was overjoyed when they arrived. Earlier years' gifts had included four jars of peanut butter and shoes with special soles that did not slip on the vertical stone paths that she walked early in the morning.

They ordered wine and an antipasto with fresh sea-food—scampi, clams and carpaccio (raw thinly sliced fish). When the generous platter arrived they toasted their good fortune and friendship.

Soon Mara disappeared under the table. Bridget and Bruno could hear her chatting in Italian with a cat. They looked at each other and read each other's minds. No "How have you been? How is the trip going? How is the family?" No, Mara stayed beneath the table. Clearly, she had reached a new level of preoccupation with cats. When she did manage to bring herself up, Mara explained to her friends that the cats around the restaurant were probably sick of fish from the lake. She had prepared for the visit by getting the extra good cuts of meat from the butcher who helps feed some of her favorite cats, and bringing it to the cats she knew she would encounter by the lake. From the sounds coming from under the table, they clearly appreciated it.

She popped her head up again soon after to complete their lunch order. They would all have freshly made pasta with sole. Indeed, it was a feast. As they ate, the three friends did get a chance to visit and share stories. The meal lasted two hours. Mara was always full of good insights about politics and human nature.

At the end of the meal, when Bruno and Bridget looked at the bill, they saw that a huge discount had been deducted from the total and the word gattara had been written at the bottom. They thanked the proprietor in their best Italian. Mara had remembered the bond she and the owner had formed over cats on a previous visit. Most Italians appreciated the gattare, although Mara told tales of the exceptions, of those who went so far as to poison cats.

They crowded their faces into Bridget's small camera's frame for a selfie photo. As they walked to the train station in a mellow mood, Bridget reminded Mara to come back to the lake. The weather was perfect. Mara hadn't needed the extra rain gear that she had packed after all.

At the Passignano station they sat on a bench. Bridget felt sad to say goodbye so quickly after hello. She wondered if she would ever see Mara again. Mara had vowed never to come back to the U.S. Bridget had pledged to Bruno not to plan any more trips out of the country until he could catch up on his glass work at home. Bridget refrained from her habit of setting the wheels in motion for the next trip before the current trip was even complete. She held in her heart the picture of them waving goodbye, her eyes welling up with tears as they boarded their separate trains.

In just a few days Bridget and Bruno would leave Monepulciano and go by train to their airport hotel in Rome, then fly back to Eugene. In truth, by this time Bridget had lost steam for their travels. It would take several months for her to be able to look back on this trip with the pleasure that would come in time. Eventually she would begin to yearn for another visit. Perhaps by that time she would be studying Italian, and for what except the next trip?

But about those last days in Montepulciano. They went to the Sunday antique market on the main street in the lower part of town. Tiny table-top enterprises displayed hand crafts or antique collections of buttons, books or jewelry. Beyond them at the lowest part of the town the porchetta truck sat alongside other food carts. Bruno and Bridget had panini and shared a glass of wine. It was still not cool enough to need a sweater. Earlier that morning, Bridget had once again put on her black cotton T-shirt as she had almost every day for the last month. She had purchased it right before the trip but it seemed desperately worn to her now. It might have been worse—it could have been a cut that wasn't flattering or something she didn't like a great deal from the beginning. She had purchased it with a gift certificate from her daughter and son-in-law for $60, an unheard of amount for Bridget to spend. But it was flattering. It was scoop necked, with ¾ sleeves and the long A-line of it came down over her hips. Still, it had become a uniform, which was disheartening to Bridget who loved to "dress" for their travels.

Later that last evening they walked to the top of the hill town and went into a palazzo now used as a small civic art gallery. The exhibit was of photos taken of the town and countryside during the 1930s as vineyards sprang up everywhere. In the black and white photos, happy sun-kissed workers carried baskets of grapes for pressing. Others in the fields shared picnics of bread, cured meats, and wine. Everyone was in good spirits for the camera. The photos were a bit grainy, giving everything the look of a long-gone era.

As the daylight was dimming Bridget and Bruno randomly chose a trattoria with outdoor seating that looked out over the valley. It was their last night in Montepulciano. Everything was excellent, as it usually was in Italy. Bridget ate somewhat absentmindedly, caught as she was between two worlds, Tuscany and her home in Oregon. The trip had been good, but she felt happy to be at the end of it. Bruno lifted his glass to make another toast. "To travel," he said. "And to home," added Bridget.

Treviglio

Bridget had anticipated that the whole family would make this 2017 trip to Italy, but it turned out this was not the right time for it. Granddaughter Gemma would be turning 10. Bridget's son Jaan and their stepdaughter Rosaria were always game to visit Italy but neither could at this time. Bridget's daughter Sarina was finishing her last term of a three-year master's program in counseling. She had fully devoted herself to school, and her success was bringing her great satisfaction. The school work and tests would not be done until June and after that she would focus on finding a job. Son-in-law John was busy traveling because of his successful music career. Bridget never pressured him to add more miles to his time away from home. So the family trip would happen at another time. Bridget could still dream about it.

It had been two-and-a-half years since Bridget and Bruno had been to Italy. After the humidity and snafus of their previous trip, she had not been quick to plan ahead. However, when news of their young friend's wedding came, she surprised even herself with how quickly she jumped at the chance to attend the sweet event.

The flight to Italy was practically empty. Bridget was able to stretch out and sleep some. Their seats were near the kitchen galley. A passenger had boarded in Eugene with three large pink boxes of Voodoo donuts. From where their seats were, they could watch their flight crew steal into the galley to sample the assortment of pastries. The flight attendants' eyes rolled like children discovering sugar for the first time.

Tired from the day and a half en route, Bridget and Bruno took a cab from the airport in Linate to Treviglio, forty minutes east of Milan and thirty minutes south of Bergamo. They checked into Hotel Treviglio, located directly across from the railway station. The hotel looked like it had been built around 1900. They generally chose to stay in hotels in the historic part of the towns they visited because they were usually near the train station and other public transportation.

At first Bridget felt disappointed in the large room furnished only with a free standing closet, one chair, and an old TV. There were floor to ceiling windows in the room and a large bathroom. Heavy wooden folding screens stood across the windows for privacy and to block out the heat of the sun. They made the plain room dark. The curtains and bedspread were new and of a shiny synthetic fabric in shades of maroon. By the time they returned later in the month for the wedding and were placed in the same room, they appreciated how large it was. By then, they had grown used to simple, older hotel furnishings.

The bridal couple, Christine and Luigi, had emailed them the names of a few dining places just a block away from their hotel that might be open, since they were arriving late in the day. They had seen Christine and Luigi a few months before, during the young couple's visit to Eugene. When Christine and her two sisters were toddlers, Bridget had taken care of them daily until they reached primary school. Bruno had known the girls' mother Patricia as a young girl. The two families shared many events together back in Eugene. One of Bridget's favorites was the annual Christmas caroling party at Patricia's.

Bridget was brimming over with happiness to be in Italy for the auspicious occasion of the wedding. The travelers found an inviting enoteca where a glass of red wine for each restored them. The jovial owner, Gabrielle, served them some fresh cut pancetta, plus local cheese and bread. Bruno, quick to use his Italian, engaged him in conversation, since they were the only ones in the small wine bar. Bridget was able to follow the conversation, asking Bruno to ask the population of Treviglio. When Gabrielle said *trenticinque mille*, she decided not to ask if he knew Christine and Luigi. She forgot that "mille" meant thousands, not millions, in Italian. Bruno mentioned the wedding, the American…and Gabrielle's face lit up. Christine had taught Gabrielle's sweetheart English, and the night before the wedding there was going to be a party at the wine bar. "Piccolo mondo," thought Bridget as they found their way back to the hotel in the dark.

Returning to the hotel and listening to the clatter of people and trains at the train station across the street, she quickly drifted off. She slept well in the double bed. That night she had a rare dream of her mother. In it, the two made a nest of blankets to sleep outside in the back yard of her childhood home above the lake. This was unlike Bridget's usual dreams and especially sweet since her mother had never slept outside or camped, two of Bridget's favorite things to do.

In the morning a disaster was averted when Bridget plugged her curling iron and adapter into the electric socket. The adapter, as it turned out, did not include a converter for Europe's different voltage requirement. She set the curler on the pillow, thinking that it wouldn't get very hot, but within seconds it burned through the pillowcase, protector and pillow. She soon noticed a nasty smell. When she lifted the curler she saw the dark burn mark; it was seconds away from a blaze. She rushed the pillow to the sink. The curling iron had fried, too. A memory came back to her. She had done this once before, in Rome, and had burned off a lock of her hair. Bruno later showed the pillow to the housekeeping staff and offered to pay for it. They were gracious and made nothing of it.

After breakfast at the hotel they took off to explore the town on foot. Just a few blocks away they located a small outdoor farmers market and picked up a jar of honey and some wine to take to dinner at Christine and Luigi's later that day. They noticed a small science education building nearby. When they entered through a side door (which wasn't the main entry) they caught the staff of two by surprise. A handful of enthusiastic senior citizens were volunteering. The displays looked like a science fair and were minimal, but that didn't dampen the curiosity of the twelve nine-year-olds on a field trip. When it was discovered that Bruno and Bridget were American, they were encouraged to greet the children in English. It was becoming very popular to study English in town. Unlike the tourist locations and larger towns, few people in Treviglio spoke English.

Bridget noticed a sign outside a café advertising a glass of wine for two euro fifty ($2.75). The restaurant, Petite Paris, turned out to be so much more than a café. The woman cooking, serving and charming the guests at the three tables resembled Bridget Bardot. She was blonde and had her hair piled up, with a few tendrils escaping. Her lips were outlined in a darker shade of lipstick and her size-four black ensemble made her look like an aging movie star. Bridget marveled as the woman accomplished everything on stiletto heels. Bruno was captivated too. She produced their lunch from a brick oven behind the small counter. They were impressed to be served *Orata* (whole fish) roasted in stewed tomatoes, lemon and white wine. Then followed roasted potatoes, salad, bread, and a plate of orange slices, strawberries, and almonds, dusted in powdered sugar, plus a bite-sized piece of dark chocolate. After an espresso, Bridget and Bruno felt ready for a nap. They took the free town shuttle from the center of the old town back to the train station and strolled across the street to their hotel.

That evening Christine met them in the hotel lobby. She bubbled with excitement and wedding details. To appreciate the neighboring residential area, they walked for twenty minutes to the couple's apartment.

Luigi had grown up in the same apartment he and Christine were living in. His father, mother, two brothers, and two grandmothers had lived in what was now plenty of room for two. Giuseppe and Maria Rosa, Luigi's parents, had retired to Giuseppe's childhood home in Liguria. Italy was currently taxing second houses and their utilities at a high rate. It was not uncommon for young people to move into a ready-made home as a work-around to avoid these taxes for the parents.

Luigi arrived from his work in the nearby town of Bergamo just as they were opening the prosecco. The four of them sampled some of the meats from the farm where the wedding feast would be held and Luigi made them risotto Milanese. Christine had made cookies, which went perfectly with strawberries and a tiny sample of Italian liqueurs. The conversation, in English, sparkled as they talked about events around the wedding. Many of the couple's friends were also getting married that spring, so they were in a whirl of social activity. Bridget felt the joy of being in Italy with people she loved.

Luigi drove them home. They all had early starts the next day. For Bridget and Bruno, it would be on a train to Venice, a city they both were looking forward to visiting again.

Venice

Bridget and Bruno unloaded their luggage and walked through the Santa Lucia train station and down the steps near the row of vaporetto stops. Just then the noon bells rang out from a nearby church. The cinematic moment was not lost on Bridget—her heart swelled to be back in Venice. Throngs of people were in line to buy vaporetto tickets. The sun was out on the cool mid-May day. Their bed and breakfast was near the Ospedale stop, so they boarded the waterbus and sat where they could keep their luggage out of the way. Ospedale was seven stops away, a satisfying tour of the lagoon.

Their two-star hotel, Alloggi Barbaria, was easy to find. Nearby was the Coop grocery store where they had shopped on a previous stay in the Castello neighborhood.

Their comfortable room was bright and clean, with two water glasses (better for wine than plastic) and good wi-fi. Bridget liked the cotton bedspread, which was worn but cool to the touch. There was a refrigerator and a table for two that would come in handy when they had picnics in the room. Bruno asked their hosts for a recommendation for lunch and they felt very lucky to find the osteria before its closing at 2 p.m. They split an order of seafood-stuffed ravioli, roasted asparagus, wine and coffee. After the memorable meal, it was a perfect time for a nap.

That evening they walked through familiar neighborhoods to find a bancomat where they could withdraw some euros. Soon they had reached St. Mark's square. Just as they arrived a group of six dinner-jacket clad musicians began playing a wonderful rendition of *Moon River*, one of Bridget's favorite songs. The tourists had thinned out, so Bridget and Bruno walked around with ease. There was no line to get into St. Mark's Basilica.

Bridget thought of all the important events that had taken place in the church—weddings, baptisms, funerals and the everyday prayers of the entire parish in this magical city plus those of the visitors from around the world. Bridget added her prayers. The richness of the art and the glass chandeliers was stunning.

The international food available implied Venice was a Muslim-friendly city, but the mosque in nearby Mestre had recently closed because of an alleged bomb threat to the Rialto Bridge. Five synagogues in Venice added to the diversity.

After visiting the cathedral, Bruno and Bridget took the vaporetto from St. Mark's all the way around the canal back to home. They passed large palazzi with sheltered canal-side boat landings. Some they knew by name, like Ca' Rezzonico, where Robert Browning and his son Pen lived for a while. Small motorboats, barges, water taxis and vaporettos skillfully slid by each other. "Would grandchild Gemma like riding the vaporetto and looking at the map?" asked Bruno. They agreed that she would love it, and that Venice would be an adventure for her. This was their sixth trip and it wouldn't be their last.

Bridget and Bruno stopped at the grocery for some food items and grappa, then settled in for the evening and watched a movie on the laptop. Bruno had never seen *Breakfast at Tiffany's*, a movie that had shaped Bridget's and many young women's notion of style in the 60's. They enjoyed the movie and the recently heard theme song, *Moon River*.

After breakfast the next morning, they took the vaporetto to visit the area around Ca' d'Oro stop. They needed to order a cappuccino to rectify the bad instant coffee at the B&B. *Ca' d'Oro* (House of Gold) a palazzo on the Grand Canal, houses a small art gallery. The exhibit, including dozens of large Oriental carpets, was from the owner's collection. The strong details of the architecture had withstood the elements over ten centuries.

What Bridget loved most were the balconies on the second and third floor looking over the Grand Canal. These were large empty spaces fit for the nobility of Venice. They lingered, resting against each other in a familiar way, and watched activity below on the water. One barge had a crew doing maintenance and replacement of rotted wood piers. They watched a handsome dog, a springer spaniel, leaping from one end of the boat to the other.

The top item on Bridget's must-do list for Venice was to cross the canal by *traghetto*, a public gondola. She had read about this in several Donna Leon mysteries, all set in Venice. The fifteen passengers sharing their public transportation gondola were a mix of residents and tourists. It took only a few minutes to cross the canal at this point, and once again Bridget's spirits soared all the way. This thrill cost 2 euros. The utilitarian gondolas cross the width of the canal. Many people stand since there are only a few seats for those who need one. The fancier gondolas that travel the length of the canal have limited seating to match their fancy fittings and price.

Bridget and Bruno wandered around the Rialto market, admiring table after table of produce and fish. Each item was perfectly arranged, as if by a food stylist. The area was crowded with tourists.

A vaporetto took them to the Giardino stop. This park, surrounding the venue for the Biennale, was at the top of Bruno's list. A week early for the international art event, they located a large empty osteria for some pizza and wine. The wait staff there were obviously immigrants, maybe from Albania or perhaps the former Yugoslavia. Bridget and Bruno had noticed the same trend in several other small businesses, including their hotel. The native population of Venice was shrinking even as tourists were growing in number.

After returning to the B&B and resting, the travelers headed to the second item on Bridget's list, the Ponte Rosso (Red Bridge) taverna. This was where Bridget and Bruno had met the retired gondolier and the glass artist in 2011. It held a special place in both of their memories of Venice. The neighbors still gathered there, though it looked like there were new owners who had redesigned the three-hundred-square-foot wine bar and seafood café. Campari spritz were a cheap two-euros-and-fifty—no wonder it had retained its charm. The three tables for four were full but Bruno and Bridget stayed, leaning against the wall. People stood around balancing small plates of fresh seafood in one hand and an aperitivo in the other. It was tricky to manage but so enjoyable.

As they walked hand in hand back through the Castello, they stopped at a shop with postcards of sketches of cats in Commedia dell'Arte costumes and bought two for Gemma. Next door was a bakery they couldn't resist. The selection of pastries was vast. Special nut cookies were wrapped with the seal of the establishment. They chose a chocolate cream torta to take home to share and a wrapped cookie to be a gift.

Thrilled and fulfilled by the events of the day, they settled into bed with a bit of grappa and a pastry to watch on Bruno's laptop an episode of *The Crown*, a series about the life of young Queen Elizabeth of England.

The next morning, refreshed and ready to fill a day that promised to be sunny and mild, they headed for a cappuccino. On the way, Bruno took Bridget's hand and said that he had a surprise for her. Winding through the *calli* (small streets off larger walking routes), they came upon the *questura* (police headquarters) that had been used as a backdrop for the Donna Leon mysteries that Bridget loved. Years before Bruno had purchased four DVDs of the series, and Bridget watched them many times. Standing in front of the entrance with the two rows of round terra cotta colored columns beside her felt like a triumph. This item on her wish list provided a moment almost too good to be true.

They got another jolt of pleasure as they settled on a café for their cappuccino and met the owner, who proudly showed them a framed photo of Barack Obama and himself standing in front of the bar. The owner, an Elvis impersonator, had caught Obama's attention when the former president visited Venice. Bridget was also amused to spy a large boxed wine, triple the size of the large "four bottle" boxes back home.

The couple enjoyed the morning sun on their faces as they walked to the vaporetto taking them to Le Stanze del

Vetro, a museum dedicated to glass on the island of San Giorgio Maggiore. Le Stanze is located in the west wing of the ex-Convitto (a former boarding school). Bridget thought it odd that the show was not on the glass island of Murano where they had stayed and visited many times.

San Giorgio is a hallowed spot, quiet and devoid of bars and commercial distractions. In their half-dozen previous visits to Venice, Bruno and Bridget had never been there. The small island was defined by the gallery, the grand San Giorgio Maggiore Church (said to be the finest monastic church in the lagoon) and a private marina. A hundred large luxury boats, inconspicuous and secluded from the masses of tourists, were docked.

Posters for the gallery's show of work by the Italian designer Ettore Sottsass had been all over Venice. Sottsass was famous world-wide for designing home furnishings under the movement called Memphis. He died in 2007. His long career included investigations into ceramics, accomplishments as an industrial designer, and a large body of designs for work in glass. This show was all about the glass, some 200 large colorful pieces.

Bruno had read that there would be a mid-day tour in English. Only one person joined them as the attractive docent led them on the semi-private stroll through Sottsass' glass designs. Bruno pointed out that glass artisans carried out Sottsass' designs while, in the American glass movement, the glass artists (such as himself) usually created designs and also took part in the production.

They left a bit dazed by the beauty of the exhibit. For Bridget, coming to Venice was synonymous with things like this—seeing small shows by world famous artists that were far beyond her dreams. They took the vaporetto back to the neighborhood near Santa Lucia and sat down in a bar for a panini and a glass of wine. While observing the locals and the tourists ordering their lunches, they struck upon the idea of taking the number one vaporetto line all the way through the Grand Canal back to the Ospedale stop. It was a slow and scenic float. The canal was already full of boats and it wasn't even high season.

That night, back in their room, they fixed plates of salad with some meats and cheeses from the Coop and watched another episode of *The Crown*. There was a sudden rain shower outside and they could hear the gentle pelting on surfaces as the bells sounded somewhere close by. The next day would be their last full day in Venice. Bridget tried not to think of this.

After breakfast, they retraced their steps to the bar of the Elvis impersonator. It was closed, so they had to settle for cappuccino next door. This day's adventure would be to revisit Casa dei Tre Oci, where they had seen a photo exhibit in 2011. Casa dei Tre Oci is a small gallery in a neo-gothic palace located on the island of Giudecca. It was at the tip of Venice where not many people traveled. It was these discoveries away from the tourist areas that they remembered so fondly.

They had not heard of the exhibiting photographer, the American David LaChapelle. Born in 1963, his thirty-year career was well represented in the gallery. The striking images were full of humor and irony. He staged each photograph in great detail. Some of his subjects included Michael Jackson, Courtney Love and a Kurt Cobain lookalike.

A previous visitor had written in the comment book "hyper-realistic aesthetic with profound social message," and this resonated with Bridget. They walked from the palazzo and stopped for a spritz and panini in a small café by the edge of the lagoon. From one of the three tables for two, they lingered a moment and watched the sun sink on the horizon. A slight breeze lifted their paper napkins off the table and Bridget's turquoise silk scarf rippled around her neck. The spot was perfect for snapping a few photos.

As they walked back slowly to their B&B to pack and prepare for tomorrow's departure, they held hands and playfully chatted about the new memories that they had made in Venice. That night they would make love after a final visit to the taverna next to the red bridge, Ponte Rosso.

Treviso and Asolo

It was afternoon when Bruno and Bridget took the short train ride to Treviso. A taxi took them to their hotel, the Residenza Domus Dotti V. The hotel's front, facing the cobblestone street, was unassuming, but their taxi driver assured them that this was the best place to stay in town. From the moment they walked through the door until their departure three days later, they could not have agreed more.

The 13th-century building had been recently converted to a bed and breakfast, with six rooms and public spaces elegantly restored. Bridget appreciated that the plumbing was high-end and modern. The free-standing glass shower had many dials and fixtures. The counters were marble and the thick bath towels came with notes informing guests that each would cost 150 euros to replace if found missing. Still, the effect of the hotel was one of fairytale comfort—the winding marble staircase, the Steinway grand piano, the ornate billiard table and game room that were all part of the hotel's public spaces. For the first night, they were the only guests. Bridget had to pinch herself to make sure she wasn't dreaming. She had found this deluxe location on a travel site and it was a splurge, yet still within their budget, at $126 a night. She wanted to ensure a pleasant place for their next visitors, two of Bruno's sisters.

Bruno and Bridget explored the town as they shopped for cured meats, local cheeses, olives, paté, and bread. They chose special wines and bubbly from the Veneto. This would be an early evening, with a picnic in the room. Bruno's sisters Maggie and Carol would arrive the next evening and stay with them at the residence for two nights.

The sisters arrived with some woeful travelers' tales to tell Bridget and Bruno. Maggie had flown from California to Sheffield, England to meet Carol, who had flown from Florida and was visiting her son and daughter-in-law and their young children. Maggie became so violently ill on the international flight that she was taken by ambulance to the hospital in Sheffield where she stayed for several days. When she was back on her feet after the gastro-intestinal knock out, the two intrepid sisters traveled to Paris, where their niece lived with her husband and infant daughter. Their visit was wonderful but not long enough for Maggie to recover. By the time they arrived in Treviso it was a miracle that Maggie was still standing. Bridget would not have blamed Maggie if she had chosen to curl up in the comfort of her palazzo room for a day or two, but Maggie was made of stronger stuff so the touring continued.

The next morning, in the beautiful dining room off the kitchen, the party of four were served a tasty breakfast. They could choose either the egg and meat plate or countless pastries. Bruno and Bridget ate like field hands and had a wonderful time catching up with the sisters and chatting with the small staff, who worked with an air of sophistication that matched the palazzo's. They learned as much as they could about a new (to them) Italian tradition, the Alpini.

On their arrival day, while strolling the city center, Bridget and Bruno had witnessed the bi-annual coming of the Alpini. These elite mountaineers, mostly men, could be recognized by their wool felt fedoras. Each was festooned with a feather (raven, eagle, goose) denoting their rank. These guards of the mountainous northern border of Italy are known for herringboning uphill on skis and then swooshing down. Alpini have a reputation as the sharpest shooters, and their bravery is legendary. A military corps of the Italian Army, they are also often the first to arrive for rescue missions after earthquakes or disasters. The order, established in 1872, fought in World Wars I and II. Currently, the national organization has 355,000 members. They maintain mountain chapels and a series of shelters for weary hikers. Soon after the four Americans were scheduled to leave, Treviso, with its population of just 85,000, would swell to accommodate 130,000 more Alpini for the weekend.

Although Bridget and Bruno always tried to attend *feste* (community celebrations) while in Italy, they were completely caught off guard and delighted by the Alpini reunion. As they set out to further explore the town, they encountered many groups of these fun-loving soldiers drinking with ebullient camaraderie. Toasting from morning until night, singing (anti-war songs, love songs, and songs about pining for home), telling stories, and riding in open-topped Jeeps or on bikes, the Alpini gave Bridget a glimpse of a new aspect of Italy to enjoy. Bruno pointed out a small dog wearing an Alpini hat and coat, and Bridget snapped a photo.

The town of Treviso is often overlooked by tourists, who opt for the more-famous Venice just to the south and a seven-euro train ride away. Treviso's many small canals and lovely old buildings with flower boxes exploding with color in May were a delight. It was easy to walk around, although the layout was confusing for Bridget, who never did get her bearings. She enjoyed watching Bruno and his sisters as they navigated the town. Both sisters remained upbeat despite the setbacks of their holiday. Carol was blond and perpetually cheerful. The health issues she had faced over the years had not affected her spirit. Maggie was tall, with light brown hair and a no-nonsense air that Bridget thought must be handy in her commercial real estate firm.

Maggie felt well enough to take the train into Venice, so on the full day of their two- night visit, the four made the trip. They managed to visit St. Marks and walk along the canal long enough to get a small taste of Venice. Later that night, back in Treviso, they located a traditional meal of the Veneto. They ordered polenta and risotto dishes that were flavored with vegetables and cheese. As sweet as the visit was, Bridget could tell that it was taking a lot of effort for Maggie to be such a good sport. The sisters flew out of Venice the next day to their homes on opposite sides of the U.S. It was touching to Bridget that their sweeping itinerary included this time spent with her and Bruno. Maggie and Carol clearly adored their big brother.

After their three nights in Treviso, Bridget and Bruno traveled a short distance north and west to Asolo, where they encountered still more small groups of Alpini setting up for the weekend's celebrations.

Both Treviso and Asolo, called The Pearl because of its aristocratic atmosphere, were destinations of Bruno's choosing. He chose Asolo because Robert Browning and his son Pen (short for Peninni), distant relatives of Bruno's, had spent some time there. In fact, Bridget and Bruno's Hotel

Duse was on Via Roberto Browning. Although the hotel was small, clean, and unremarkable, the hosts, Signore Vito and Signora Isabella, were exceedingly warm to their American guests. Bridget was amused to be hugged to pieces at every opportunity and kissed on both cheeks by Signora Isabella. Vito and Isabella were busy managing the hotel's twenty rooms. The signora was a very energetic octogenarian who spoke proudly of hiking uphill to the castle every day. This was something Bruno did in every town with a castle. His hike usually presented Bridget a good opportunity to rest.

Encouraged to do so by their new best friends, Vito and Isabella, the travelers took a day trip to Bassano del Grappa. The 65-euro cab fare was a splurge. Legend has it that a Roman soldier invented the strong drink in the second century, and the town is the home of grappa's most famous distilleries, plus a museum dedicated to its history. To their surprise, they discovered the town also made aquavit, the Scandinavian digestivo flavored with caraway seeds.

Bridget and Bruno had their sips of grappa (they did not swig it) followed by a nice lunch along the Brenta River with a view of the famous bridge, Ponte degli Alpini, designed by Andrea Palladio in 1569. The bridge, a covered wooden pontoon expanse, was under restoration but still open. As they walked over it they encountered a large group of Alpini being led in song by a young woman and an older man. Spirits ran high. There was a lot of toasting and at the other end of the bridge, a wedding party had made this town a destination on their special day. Bridget always loved to see young Italians dressed to the nines and celebrating.

They walked back through a newer part of town filled with shops that were chic but not as high-end as Dolce & Gabbana or Prada, the shops you would see in Naples,

Florence, Rome, or Milan. Among the shops in Bassano they saw the Oregon Shop, something they had never seen before in Italy. It had the most boring, mono-colored clothes! They were not only drab, they were rumpled! They laughed and agreed that the Northwest did indeed value function over fashion.

Three nights was just enough time to scratch the surface of small towns like Treviso and Asolo. There was the arrival day, a day to explore, a day for a small excursion out of town, and a departure day. Bridget was excited at the thought of their next location, the town of Stresa on Lago Maggiore—a place that had been her pick and where they would spend six days on the water.

Stresa on Lago Maggiore

At the graceful little town of Stresa on Lago Maggiore, Bruno and Bridget took a cab from the small train station to their hotel, Albergo Sempione. Their unremarkable third-floor room was small, with old furnishings and one window. The bed was comfortable enough and there was a bench for one suitcase. French doors opened to a balcony barely big enough for a bistro table and two chairs. They luckily discovered a small store with great takeout lasagna, pastas, roasted vegetables, meats, and wines for their many picnics on the balcony facing the courtyard below. The balcony offered a view of other terraces and balconies that were never occupied.

The front of the hotel boasted a neon sign that read *Ristorante Sempione*. The sign was never lit, maybe because the dining space was used only to serve breakfast to the overnight guests. Unlike their small room, the dining room was a sun-filled jewel with wall-to-wall windows facing the lake and the ferry station, the main hub for travel on the lake. Tablecloths lent the dining room a formal air; attentive wait staff greeted them each morning. The buffet offered an expansive selection of cheese, coffee, cured meat, yogurt, muesli, and pastries. Bridget and Bruno were grateful that they were not on some scheduled tour and so could have a second cappuccino and take their time getting out the door in the morning.

Being in this small resort town was as peaceful as Bridget had hoped it would be. Everywhere she looked she saw the freshness of springtime. The sun glistened on the water and the distant snow-capped mountains. In the six nights they would be there they would have time to unpack, check in with folks back home, and do some shopping. Bridget managed to get the lay of the land quickly. The water not only brought her great pleasure to view, it was a sure point of orientation.

Lago Maggiore and Lago di Como are the lakes closest to Milan. In 1906, tunneling of the Simplon Pass allowed trains north of the Alps to arrive in Stresa. In fact, Simplon in Italian is *Sempione*, the name of their hotel. Lago Maggiore has magnificent architecture on several of its islands and the public is free to visit them by boat. There were several large and grand hotels built in the Liberty style (Arte Nouveau), a nearby funicular, lakeside dining, and a good amount of shopping.

Lago Maggiore is Italy's longest lake. Lake Garda, further east, is the largest and is popular for outdoor pursuits like hiking, sailing, biking, windsurfing, and kite boarding. Garda has dramatic beauty, with cliffs steeper than those of the Amalfi Coast facing the deep blue water. Lago di Como has a fancy feeling, where one of the main activities for tourists is strolling along and gazing at stately mansions while trying to catch a glimpse of the George and Amal Clooney family.

On their first day of exploring Stresa, Bruno and Bridget enjoyed visiting the small shops. They popped into a shop selling imported things that was a bit of a jumble but called to Bridget. She bought two cotton scarves made in India for gifts. They headed north, outside of town, toward their destination, the Mattarone cable car. Along the lake were large fancy hotels with roof top bars and valet parking, some built long ago, others newer.

Since it was May and still off-season, there was no line to get on board the small funicular pod, the first of two that would take them up the mountain. After the second funicular, Bruno chose to travel to the very top by ski lift, leaving Bridget at a restaurant that was conveniently placed for those travelers not bold enough to venture further. While she waited, she happily ordered a Campari spritz that was accompanied by a plate of cicchetti, those tasty tapa-like bites.

Perched high above the lake, Bridget's mind roamed. All winter she had been plagued with plantar fasciitis on the soles of both feet. She wasn't able to walk much to prepare for the trip. Instead, she had a series of acupuncture treatments to quiet the inflammation and she wore ugly but sensible shoes. The two or three miles that she and Bruno had just walked represented an accomplishment to her. Being able to walk throughout the trip was a great relief. Bruno had been good about slowing down. Bridget, not being crabby because of heat and humidity like their trip to the south of Italy two years earlier, felt it was going well. As always, with three weeks out and one remaining, she was feeling pangs of homesickness for their grown kids and grandchild. Bridget checked her cell phone and was able to connect to Facebook and her messages.

Bruno returned with beautiful photos of the Alps. In Oregon, they were accustomed to foothills, buttes, and mountains, but even the peaks of the Cascade Range are nothing like the Alps.

Bruno and Bridget descended by funicular, enjoying a spectacular view of the seven blue lakes and the Po Valley. They chose to take a short ferry ride home rather than walk again in front of the lakeside hotels. Bridget was happy to be on the water. Before she knew it, they were at their hotel. She knew there would be more ferry rides. They picked up some cheese and vegetables for a salad and late dinner on their balcony and ended the day with more of *The Crown* streamed on Bruno's laptop.

The next day they took advantage of the sun and an early start. They would travel by ferry and visit two of the three Borromeo Islands, Isola Madre and Isola Bella. The boat was not crowded so they had their choice of seating—inside, on top, or up front on the boat. Bridget loved the wind blowing against her face on the top level. She snuggled next to Bruno for warmth. He tenderly put his arm around her and smiled as their day and the boat picked up speed.

The gardens of the palaces on Isola Bella and Isola Madre were jaw-dropping botanical wonders built on terrace upon terrace. The grounds of Isola Madre had a collection of birds living on the nineteen acres of English-style gardens. White peacocks captivated the picture-snapping tourists as the birds roamed freely. Inside both castles, Bridget saw the biggest collection of marionettes and stages for productions she had ever seen. Room after room was stuffed with props, costumed puppets, and tools of stagecraft. All of it, Bridget mused, must have provided great entertainment for royalty who visited the grand palazzi. The exhibit demonstrated the Italians love of play and didn't shy away from scary themes like monsters and hell. She wondered if some productions were just for adults?

The palaces were enormous. The royals of Monte Carlo from the house of Grimaldi tried to purchase one of the islands but learned quickly it was not for sale. When Princess Diana and Prince Charles of Wales visited, Diana requested dinner in the ballroom. The ballroom was an enormous marble wonder, with bench seating against the walls circling a room as large as you might see in a palazzo in Venice. The benches were covered in pale pink satin that was topped with a clear plastic slipcover. This made Bridget smile. She wondered if the slipcovers had been removed for the meal served to Charles and Diana.

In the garden of Isola Bella the couple splurged on a fancy cheese plate and glass of wine. The plate was done well, with reasonable sized samples of three cheeses, gorgonzola, fontina, and taleggio, and bread. The white wine was cool and crisp in the warmth of the late afternoon.

Later the couple boarded the ferry, choosing to circle the islands again and watch the sun sink in the sky. They observed a well-chaperoned group of middle-school students wearing the latest in hairstyles, girls with sections of their hair artfully shaved on one side or halfway up the back and boys with their own versions. Laughter and high spirits filled the fresh air off the lake.

It was late when they got back to the hotel. They walked five blocks to the Coop supermercato to pick up items for another dinner on the balcony. On the way back they stopped at their new favorite *alimentari* (deli), to pick up some special wine and cheese.

The couple spent the next morning hand washing laundry and hanging it by any available means, utilizing the balcony but being careful not to have hung clothing items visible to others. Later they popped in and out of shops and treated themselves to a lovely lunch. Their friend Angela had told them of a restaurant she and her husband Jerry had enjoyed while visiting the previous year. It was next door to Hotel Sempione and did not disappoint them. Bruno had polenta and osso buco and Bridget had her favorite, a huge bowl of mussels steamed in white wine, garlic and butter, with a side of roasted vegetables.

After lunch, the couple strolled along the lake and stopped at the train station to buy tickets for their big adventure the next day. They would travel up through the Alps to Locarno, Switzerland and return by ferry over the entire length of the lake. They then picked up some roasted vegetables and pasta for a light meal at the end of another lovely day. Bridget again thought to herself how much she enjoyed these easy days of travel. She pondered what was ahead on their remaining days. They would be on the lake for two more nights, then back to Treviglio for four nights to experience the crown jewel of the trip, Christine and Luigi's wedding. After that they would wrap up their four weeks of travels with four nights in Turin and one night just outside of Milan near the Linate airport.

The first train they boarded the next day took them to Domodossola. From there they rode the blue narrow gauge train known as the Centovalli Railway that runs through "a hundred valleys." It was a breathtaking ride across the border and through some of Switzerland's most magnificent mountain scenery. The train trundled slowly over precarious viaducts that spanned seemingly bottomless ravines. Plunging waterfalls appeared regularly. A poster inside the train noted that they would cross eighty-three bridges and travel through twenty tunnels during the three-hour ride.

They hopped off the train mid-trip in the town of Santa Maria Maggiore, hoping to visit the Chimney Sweep Museum, the only one of its kind in the world. Unfortunately, the museum was closed. They both had been looking forward to learning the history of chimney sweeps and the stories of the many men, women, and children who emigrated to the big cities in winter from Germany, Switzerland, and Scandinavia starting in the sixteenth century. Santa Maria itself was a tiny city. Bruno and Bridget had to appease themselves by taking photos of the life-size metal silhouettes of several different sweeps on top of the buildings. The sweeps stood in fanciful poses, plying their trade. Every year in September, Bridget later learned, a three-day Chimney Sweep Festival and parade was held in the area, where alpine homes had roofs made from local stone (gneiss rock) and extremely tall chimneys.

The next train from Santa Maria took them into Switzerland. As soon as they arrived they looked for a place for lunch and settled on outdoor seating at a restaurant in a busy section of the town not too far from where they would board the ferry. The panino Bridget ordered was mediocre and expensive, and the waitperson treated them with an air of indifference. This was the northern country of her grandmother's family, the Neichwanders, who came from Bern. Decades ago her mother's sisters had visited relatives there and reported they were as stern as the aunts they remembered from their childhood in Ohio.

After lunch, on their visit to a Lindt chocolate store, Bridget and Bruno decided that the prices for the same chocolate were better back home. Bruno had the urge to explore, and Bridget was happy to sit in the sun at the ferry station and read for a few hours, waiting for their four-hour boat trip back to Stresa.

The ferry was larger than the others they had been on when traveling around the Borromeo Islands. It had an inside room large enough for many tables and chairs, and a bar with snacks on the upstairs level. After a while the landscape took on a sameness, in contrast to the train ride. The time flew by, though, because Bruno and Bridget chatted with other tourists. They met a couple from Medford, Oregon, enjoying their first trip to Italy. The day was sunny and cool. The ride was smooth. Bridget felt the bitter sweetness of arriving at the dock in Stresa for the last time.

The sense of having done and seen it all came over her. Back at the hotel, she and Bruno finished their remaining picnic snacks, pulled their belongings together, and went to bed hoping for a good night's sleep. The next day's travels would have them return to Treviglio in time for the young couple's Italian/American style prenuptials.

The Wedding

THE AMERICANS ARRIVE

Bruno and Bridget returned to the same hotel and the very room that they had occupied at the beginning of their trip. Several other wedding guests were also staying at this hotel. A total of thirteen Americans had descended on Treviglio (a town not mentioned in most guide books) for Christine and Luigi's wedding.

As soon as they arrived, Bridget and Bruno encountered Margaret, their longtime friend from Eugene. She was a welcome sight, waving from her room's balcony. Margaret was an upbeat and energetic woman who had known the bride's mother, Patricia, for decades, and had given jobs to the bride's two sisters, Ellen and Claire, at the University of Oregon food services.

Bruno, Bridget and Margaret walked together from the hotel to the rental of the bride's immediate family. They were staying in a spacious and well-appointed home that occupied several levels of a palazzo that had bedrooms and bathrooms for seven.

Bridget thought of the bride and her sisters, Claire and Ellen, as three individualistic, and yet all sweet, young women with definite similarities and devotion to each other. Bridget had known them well from toddler to kindergarten age because they were in her care most days at the day school she owned and ran in Eugene.

The bride's parents, George and Patricia, were surprisingly calm, given that they were about to co-host an Italian/American wedding. They had carried sixty pounds of goods in their luggage—the wedding dress, food imports (including twenty pounds of carefully packed smoked salmon), and gifts from friends and family who could not make the trip. Christine, Claire, and Ellen were absorbed in creating table decorations and other flourishes for the wedding and reception, while brother-in-law Jesse was upstairs rehearsing his guitar introduction for the ceremony.

Not wanting to disrupt their focus or be in the way, the visitors headed back to their hotel and made plans to meet up with the bride's family later that evening. Years before, Bruno and Bridget had enjoyed travel in Italy with George and Patricia over an Easter holiday. In Eugene they had spent many evenings together. Their Eugene homes were just a few blocks from each other. Bruno and Bridget had visited Christine in Milan the first year that she lived in Italy, even before she had met Luigi.

The travelers first official wedding event was a meet-up held at the wine bar they had visited at the start of their trip. After the rehearsal and meal the members of the wedding party joined the American guests for a first toast and mingle. The romantically lit wine bar was full of happy people. Bruno was key to this event and the ones that followed because some of the groom's family were not fluent in English, nor were many people in the small town. Most of the visitors from the states were not Italian speakers either.

Free flowing wine soon loosened tongues enough to foster a merging, with some phrases being understood and many a miss amid the happy smiles and high spirits for the young couple. The sparkling glances and the great joy of the wedding couple were sweet; their wit was quick and lively. Luigi was dark haired and Christine had light-brown locks that were long and straight. Both were trim and full of health. Bridget smiled, thinking of this couple on the brink of a very big step and sensing they were ready.

The morning after the meet-up, Bruno and Bridget enjoyed several cappuccini at nearby Paolo Riva Café, known for its assortment of pastries, and then spent the rest of the morning dressing for the wedding. Bruno had been studying YouTube instructional videos to learn how to tie his white bow tie and had perfected it just in time. There were bow ties galore at the wedding, some made by the bride's sisters. Bridget added a colorful scarf to her black formal shirt and black and white striped culottes.

Downstairs they met Margaret, who was flustered because her sandal had broken. With the notion of *bella figura* (making the best impression visually) in mind, she asked Bruno if he thought they could find a shoe repair on Saturday morning between the hotel and the civic building where the ceremony would take place. Fat chance, thought Bridget, but Bruno had already "mounted his white horse." Navigating the language, he found a tailor at the second shop they tried and persuaded her to do some fast stitching. Bridget grew impatient waiting for the repair to be made. They were close enough to the wedding event that she could see some of the groom's family standing outside. Afraid of missing a moment of the big day, Bridget ran ahead and found a seat in the room used for ceremonies.

Margaret and Bruno arrived soon after, in plenty of time for the start of the wedding.

The Italian/American Wedding and Reception

The bride and her family walked to the civic center, the town's historic architecture providing the perfect backdrop for the photos snapped along the way by the photographer.

Christine Marshall entered the room on the arm of her father and climbed the steps to its small stage. Everyone stood so they could see her better. She beamed and, as usual, appeared calm. George, well composed in spite of the emotions easily read on his face, was giving his daughter to a worthy young man, Luigi Ricco, and to Italy. The radiant mother, Patricia, took her seat in the front row next to the groom's attractive parents, Maria and Giuseppe. The two witnesses and officiant, with an Italian tri-color sash across his chest, took their places.

The bride was perfection, "a little slice of heaven." She wore a tea length dress with a scooped neck and low scooped back revealing the most delicate of tattoos. The dress was fitted perfectly to Christine's tiny waist and petite form. The geometric lace pattern over the off-white brocade came to just below the knee, and then a layer of white tulle fell from the waist to a few inches below the hem. Bridget had never before seen a dress like this, and she frequently read wedding magazines. Christine's hair was French braided from the front into a chignon surrounded by yellow daisies with baby's breath. She carried a bouquet of lemon yellow calla lilies. Luigi wore a dark suit with a teal blue bow tie.

In Italy, whether a couple gets married in a church, garden, or home, the celebrants must begin with a civic ceremony such as this one. All weddings commit first to Italian law and then, if they wish, to each other again in the church. Also, brides in Italy keep their maiden name. Bridget was taken with the words Christine and Luigi exchanged. This passage in particular struck her:

Article 143

Rights and Reciprocal Duties of the Spouses
Upon marrying, the husband and wife acquire the same rights and assume the same responsibilities. The state of matrimony entails the mutual obligation of fidelity, moral and material assistance, collaboration in the interests of family and cohabitation. Both of the spouses are obliged, each in relation to their own means and ability to work outside or inside the home, to contribute to the needs of the family."

The bride's sisters and the groom's uncle read poetry by Roy Croft and Pablo Neruda, respectively, and the newly minted brothers-in-law provided classical guitar and piano music. The eleven-year-old niece and eight-year-old nephew of the groom served as ring bearers. The mayor even made an appearance, plunking himself in the middle of the ceremony even though the couple had tried to discourage him from attending.

Bridget felt a rush of mixed emotions. She adored weddings and felt they were holy, but she felt guilt over her own lack of success at marriage. This usually made her feel uneasy at weddings, but this wedding left her with a peaceful feeling. It had been well thought out, not overdone, and mindfully focused.

Bruno and Bridget rode to the reception with childhood friends of the groom. They were a stunning couple, both rocket scientists who were working and living in France. They seemed so young to Bridget. Their car was among the first to arrive at the reception site, Podere Montizzolo, a small farm established in 1668.

The farm had been owned by the same family for centuries. The newest building had an upscale bottega featuring artisan meats and cheeses (and wine of course) which came entirely from the working farm. The trattoria seated the eighty guests comfortably and the outside courtyard was great for the games and dancing that would later spill out under the stars.

When the farm wasn't being reserved for special events the large outdoor area, with its eight grilling stations and picnic tables circling a well-equipped playground, provided enjoyment for families wanting to experience the rural tradition of the Po Valley.

The first plate was a buffet of thinly sliced meats cured at the farm. There were special cheeses from all over the world. The twenty pounds of smoked salmon from the northwest disappeared quickly. Another of Luigi's childhood friends brought an abundance of wine from his Tuscan vineyard.

When they sat down to eat, plate after plate, including vegetarian selections, arrived. They were served pasta with tomato confit and prosciutto crudo. Next came asparagus risotto with pancetta, followed by lemon and herb ham with more vegetables. The last plate was a green salad with strawberries, goat cheese, and red onion. Bridget and Bruno joined the other guests in groaning with full-belly pleasure.

Later in the afternoon a buffet of fruit, cheese and salami was provided as a snack.

Before cake cutting, desserts and more toasts came. They played games fashioned after television shows that Bridget recognized and knew were popular. She and Bruno were chosen by the bridal couple to be among five couples to compete in the dance contest. When they were called to the floor Bruno kept insisting to Bridget that they were calling only him, which made no sense at all. He insisted again. Bridget was amused and flabbergasted that he thought he might not need her on the dance floor. Bruno was never puffed up like this. They danced to four or five songs. Bridget knew how to move her feet very fast within the framework of Bruno's lead step. He had no idea. They won second place. She had to sit down for a while and catch her breath after all the wine and dancing! Guests took turns putting on hats, mustaches, and funny costumes as the wedding photographer snapped away.

While seated to enjoy the cake, the bride's aunt Anne tapped her glass with a fork and the bridal couple kissed again, honoring an American tradition. Bridget and Bruno weren't the last to leave but stayed late into the night. They both agreed they had never taken part in such a celebration in Italy and were full to bursting with all the good feelings from the special moments of this day.

Everything about the ceremony and the reception at the podere, the hours of food, wine, and merriment, would remain with Bridget forever. Christine and Luigi planned to have another less formal reception in Eugene in August of the next year for the people who were unable to make this epic trip.

The next day Bridget and Bruno traveled by train to have lunch with relatives of their son-in-law John in the nearby

town of Limito. This meeting also promised to be remarkable, because it was rare for them to have connections with
Italians when they traveled.

They were now four weeks into their trip. Bridget began
to feel weary from the travel and their social schedule. The
memories stored in her heart, however, would last a lifetime.

Torino

Bruno and Bridget's trip to Italy was winding down. They were in the last town they would visit, the large city of Torino, the home of FIAT, of Guido Gobino (maker of artisan Italian hot chocolate), of Italy's oldest permanent collection of modern art at the Galleria d'Arte Moderna, and of many other museums. Torino, the capital of Piemonte, had been Bruno's pick along with stays in Treviso and Asolo. Bridget's choices were four days in Venice, and five in Stresa, on Lago Maggorie.

Bridget enjoyed spending the time in Torino's Hotel Taverna Dantesca, staying out of the sun and off her feet. Only the "EL" of the neon "HOTEL" letters were illuminated. From the outside the hotel was shabby looking, but inside things were clean and well run. It was also inexpensive. In all the hotels of this type that they stayed in during their travels Bridget quickly adjusted to the size of their room, large or small. Most had wi-fi that worked.

Bruno had done a good job during this trip of honoring her request not to leave every afternoon to zip around with his frisky energy. He also lent a hand with her luggage when he could. Bridget had kept up remarkably well, considering that for the month before the trip she could hardly walk and, in fact, she had refrained from walking. They took a few more taxis than on previous trips. Except for a few rainy days they had enjoyed good weather. Bruno had been good about resting in the evenings, too. They generally didn't go out at night. Having a laptop filled with downloaded movies was similar to their evening routine at home. Any concern that Bridget had felt leading up to the trip had evaporated.

On the first full day, the hop-on hop-off bus gave them an overview of Torino, its mixed styles of architecture, the outlying Juventus soccer stadium and the huge FIAT plant featuring a race-track on the roof. One afternoon Bridget did rest while Bruno made his way to the FIAT auto museum. In 1899, Giovanni Agnelli, with several investors, founded the Fabbrica Italiana Automobili Torino (FIAT) Società.

The couple rode the double decker bus through neighborhoods of gently rolling hills that rose near Torino's monuments and basilicas. A 19th century tower, Mole Antonelliana, dominated the skyline. It was originally built as a synagogue, but construction was halted when costs went beyond budget. Later the tower was added, making it as tall as the Eiffel Tower, and for a time it was the tallest building in the world and served as a symbol of Italian unity. It now housed the National Museum of Cinema. Their bus guide (by way of an earphone system) pointed out the mosques, synagogues and churches side by side. Torino was a city that was proud of its diversity. It had a rich history of welcoming workers from all over the world. After WWII, the production of automobiles at the FIAT plant brought Italy out of poverty just as the fashion industry in Milan helped the country turn the corner. Torino was sometimes called the cradle of Italian liberty.

Their hotel was across a busy street and a block away from the large train station. Bruno and Bridget learned that they could walk quickly into town on the Via Roma. The shops would get fancier as they got near the grand Piazza Vittorio Veneta, the largest square in Europe. Throughout their stay they enjoyed many espressos and aperitivos sitting in the warm spring sun. They enjoyed discovering tiny neighborhood cafés. Not far from their hotel was a buffet, the Brek ristorante self service, which is a rare concept in Italy. They had several noon meals there. Pasta was cooked as they waited and they choose from dishes and sides that had nearly the same standards of excellence that a trattoria would have. Self-serve came at a considerable savings.

On day two, their tour of the Cinema museum was a treat for both of them. They especially liked films with Italian origins. Many of them were familiar to Bridget and Bruno because they crossed over into the film history of the U.S. Movie posters, film clips, reproduced sets, and amazing creative displays focusing on every part of the film craft filled the three story space. Stars like Charlie Chaplin, Fred Astaire, Ginger Rogers, Paul Newman, Sophia Loren, Anna Magnani, Marcello Mastroianni, and Audrey Hepburn were larger than life in Italy as well as in America.

On their last day they went shopping at a branch of Rinascente, a department store they had also visited in Milan, Florence, and Rome. They shopped for a birthday gift for Sallie, who had enjoyed Rinascente with them in Florence. There, thirteen years earlier, the trio had enjoyed a lunch on the rooftop with one of the best views of the city. On this day Bruno and Bridget purchased a set of espresso spoons which they could easily carry home and mail to her. The couple walked around admiring the displays, despite the high prices.

Around town they had noticed large posters advertising an exhibit of photojournalism from the archives of La Stampa, the oldest newspaper in Italy. The show, which was a one hundred and fifty year celebration, was on the ground floor of an enormous palazzo. Areas of the floor were glass to reveal the Roman ruins of a foundation of the building on the same site. Bridget and Bruno looked at each front page, dating back to World War I. There were about 100 front pages on display. The choices held a significance. Bridget's heart swelled as she took in the photos. Good photojournalism artfully captures the spirit of the time. The Italians love of fun, their caring for one another, love of soccer, and their history in turmoil shone through. There were images of the Pope, of John and Yoko Lennon, and of Barack Obama about to accept his presidential win, striding across the stage with young Sasha holding his hand. This iconic moment was already imprinted on Bridget's memory, but seeing it amplified gave her a surge of joy.

Later that day they carefully chose a small bar for their last Campari spritz. The next day they would train to Rome, where they would stay in a hotel near the airport for their early morning departure. It was always a mammoth journey to get back to the west coast of the United States.

The ending of a trip to Italy was always bittersweet for Bridget. She longed to be back with family and friends. She missed Sarina, John, grandchild Gemma, and Rosaria in Portland Oregon, and Jaan in Charlottesville, Virginia. They were her joy. Condo life in Eugene was ordered and easy. But she knew, soon enough, she would miss Italy.

Italy 2019

In the early months of 2018, Bridget designed their 2019 trip to Italy. During the rainy winter, fighting off the blues, she would sit in front of the computer and visit Italian websites and compare airline fares. Planning the trip was a source of entertainment, lifting her spirits.

She found a deal on the travel site, Gate 1, for an unescorted tour that included rail transport between Venice, Florence, and Rome, and seven nights in four-star hotels. As she and Bruno had done before, they could tack on additional weeks of travel after the tour ended so they could have an extended stay in Florence. They would land in Venice and fly back from Rome, all for the price of an average airfare. Bridget jumped on it. She found a Florence apartment in the San Frediano neighborhood that would accommodate five and booked it for a month. Bruno assured her that they would be happy with the location, which was six or seven blocks away from Santo Spirito where they had stayed for a month on three other occasions.

Because of the tight schedule of the Gate 1 itinerary, she knew that they would spend only one full day in Venice and Florence. That allowed little time for exploration at the leisurely pace she liked to travel. Two full days in Rome was slightly longer but Bridget anticipated taking her time to adjust after the flight. She could putter in the hotels and Bruno would be able to be out exploring at his speed. She could join him later in the day.

Leaving the country for a break was a healthy thing, Bridget thought. She believed that history would show that oppression grew daily during the Trump presidency. How many times did people say that it couldn't get worse, and then it did? Day after day Bridget hung on the news, hoping for some relief. Advances in education, science, and the humanities were being shredded and it was a puzzle to know how to stop Trump's reign of terror on America and its standing in the world. Should the resistance fight for impeachment or wait until the election? It was clear that the 2016 election had been compromised by manipulation of the news service and social media. It could happen again.

Why anyone supported Trump was a mystery to Bridget. She had little patience and growing contempt for Trump and the GOP who were responsible for so many dastardly deeds. Paramount in her mind, to date, was the separation of thousands of children at the border with Mexico and the failure to collect the information needed to reunite them with their families following months in tent cities with abusive conditions. Thousands of children were suffering, and it tormented Bridget to see how low her country's government had stooped.

As time inched toward the trip, Bridget and Bruno were not feeling excited. They both felt a reluctance to leave—for Bridget it was family and friends and for Bruno, work. She would miss praying with her sweet parish at St. Mary's Episcopal Church. She watched the date to cancel without penalty go by. They discussed dropping the trip, but because some friends were planning to visit and had purchased plane tickets, they stuck to their plan. Who knew how future travel might be affected by the shifting attitudes in the U.S., Great Britain, and Europe? There was a shocking power grab by the extreme right in places around the globe. Bridget felt homesick before even leaving. She would also miss the bathtub and her water pic. Was this what turning seventy was like?

As they drove up I-5, Bridget messaged Jaan, who was in Charlottesville, to say that she was "traveling to Portland with meatballs." Sensing her lagging spirit, Jaan messaged back, "Mom, that's not a very nice nickname for Bruno." His wit could always make her laugh.

The night before their flight from Portland, they shared meatballs and stayed with Sarina, John, and Gemma. Bridget appreciated the chance for a family dinner before leaving.

The next day, as the taxi arrived to take them to the airport, Sarina stood on her front porch and hugged and kissed them both. When Bridget looked back through the car window she saw her daughter nod her head up and down as if to say "yes." Bridget felt like a preschooler on the first day of child care, leaving a parent who was signaling that everything was going to be all right. The gesture reassured her.

The flight was long, with stops in Detroit, Michigan and Paris. Perhaps because she drank the wine and took a sleeping pill, it was completely forgettable.

Bridget had arranged for a water taxi to pick them up from the airport in Venice and bring them to a spot close to their hotel. She expected to be discombobulated from the flight and felt this was the simplest way to arrive for their short two night stay. They boarded the six-passenger boat and sat toward the front. She delighted in every minute of seeing Venice on this grey St. Patrick's Day and her heart swelled with pleasure on the lagoon, approaching the Cannaregio *sestiere* (neighborhood) through the Grand Canal. The boat pulled into the dock for private taxis, and finding their hotel was as smooth as silk. Maybe their reluctance to leave home would melt away, and they'd gain the respite and renewal they so often found in Italy.

Dashing Through Venice, Florence and Rome

VENICE

Bridget and Bruno settled into their room at Hotel Amadeus. The third floor window offered a lovely view of the large interior courtyard. Bridget was happy not to be facing the busy street with its many souvenir vendors just outside the hotel's front door. Taking their first stroll, they were by the canal in no time. It was before the tourist season had begun and only a few people were walking along the canal in the cool spring weather.

They found a bar for a light dinner and shared small plates of open-faced panini. "Excellent," thought Bridget. One had a heavenly soft cheese and the other a fish spread. They ordered an *ombra* (a small glass of wine) that cost 3 euros—the exchange rate made it $3.36. It was early enough in the evening that the tiny café was empty when they arrived. It was near the water but no windows faced the canal. Looking across the small table at each other, they shared a toast to a moment of joy as it registered in their hearts that they were back in Italy. This would be an early night for the couple because Bruno planned to join in the Gate 1 walking tour at 9 a.m. As they strolled home, Bridget felt content to be in one of her favorite cities. Venice was as magical this day as it always was for her. In the morning they would eat the hotel's breakfast together. Then Bridget would rest from the long plane ride while Bruno toured.

They slept well and woke with gratitude for the smooth beginning to their travels. It hadn't always been that way for Bridget, who was affected by jet lag, sometimes for over a week. After Bruno left she fussed over her hair. Over the last two years it had grown white in the front, with a little grey remaining in the rest of her short bob. "Good enough," she thought as she dressed warmly for the day.

While she waited for Bruno to return, Bridget ventured outside. They were in the Cannaregio neighborhood, just a five-minute walk to the train station. She headed in the other direction, carefully counting the five small bridges she crossed so she could retrace her steps. When it started to rain, she stopped in the Santuario di Lucia, entering the church with reverence. She let her eyes adjust to the dark interior. Bridget felt chilly and didn't stay long, wanting to get back to their cozy hotel room before she got too wet.

When he returned, Bruno told her how the tour group had taken the vaporetto to the island of Murano and visited a glass factory and show room. Several years before, the couple had stayed in a hotel on Murano for a week. Bruno, a glass artist, had visited the island's glass factories and fancy showrooms during other trips and usually chose to see other exhibitions of glass while in Venice. This time he gladly went along with the tour for the exercise, even though he did not learn anything new.

On his complimentary walking tour, Bruno had also managed to learn of a new department store, T Fondaco dei Tedeschi, on the Grand Canal next to the Rialto Bridge. This was not far from their hotel and something new for them to see. Tiles and signs on the walls of many tiny walkways had arrows to point the way to the famous Rialto, so the new store was easy to find.

The six-story building was erected in 1228 for the German (Tedeschi) merchants of the city. Fondaco is Arabic for "store house." In the 20th century, the building housed the Poste Italiano. It was sold in 2008. The subsequent conversion took years, transforming it into a posh department store with a huge atrium and a rooftop terrace. They looked down from the top floor to the ground floor restaurant with its black and white marble floor and potted palm trees, enjoying a feast of elegance.

Bridget and Bruno were not shoppers, but they admired the store's architecture and the opulent clothing displays where store personnel watched every move of the potential customers. From the top floor they took an escalator to the rooftop to take in the grand panorama of Venice. It was cool and windy on the roof. Huddling close to be warm, they swooned at the view but didn't stay long.

While searching for a café, they stumbled upon a church, Chiesa di San Giovanni Crisostomo. Bridget had yet to light a candle, and the church's unassuming entrance beckoned. It looked ancient and intriguing. She lit a long skinny taper, placed it in the candleholder, then knelt in a pew to pray. She thought of the image of Mary of Guadalupe, patron Saint of Mexico, that was displayed above the rows of candles in red glass holders in her church back home. She lit a candle every chance she got for the health and safety of her family, especially Sarina, her first born, so sensitive and bright. Sarina and Jaan's father, David, had died unexpectedly in his sleep less than a year before. Jaan was left with a staggering amount of work to settle the estate in Charlottesville, Virginia; Sarina was left with a painful void. Bridget had made peace with her memories of her first husband years ago. Now she ached and prayed for her children and the challenges they were facing in their late forties, even beyond the sudden death of their father.

It was 4 p.m. and a posted notice declared that the church would close at 4:30. Out of the corner of her eye, Bridget watched as a dour layperson marched in, swooped up all the candles in her arms as if they were long-stemmed flowers, then blew out the dozen candles all in one breath. Next she went to Bridget's freshly lit candle in its tiered group and did the same. Bruno could tell that Bridget was horrified; Bridget took her candle-lighting seriously. He spoke to the church-lady in Italian, explaining that la donna had just lit the candle and was still praying! Hearing this, the worker snatched a tamped candle, thrust it toward him, and took off to the rest of her chores.

A few hours later Bridget emailed her friend Lana, who worked at her parish in Eugene, and described this disruptive though humorous event. Her friend said that she would immediately light a candle for Bridget, promising her it would not be blown out.

The couple had memories from previous trips. They had toured many of the islands by vaporetto. They had watched enchanted couples share meals along the lagoon and had become familiar with neighborhoods, alive with generations enjoying the outdoor spaces. Bridget appreciated the way the Italians, faces lit with smiles, did ordinary activities.

The couple found an inviting café for an early dinner. Once again they shared plates of bruschetta and small glasses of wine. They would be up early the next morning, take advantage of their hotel's ample breakfast buffet of sweet and savory choices, and would head to the Santa Lucia train station for their ride to Florence.

Florence

At Venice's Santa Lucia station, Bridget and Bruno recognized others traveling in their group and joined them for a final gaze at the canal. It was always a pleasure to arrive or depart from this point, with its wall of glass just yards away from the water.

The train ride went quickly. Arriving at Santa Maria Novella Station in Florence, Bridget was grinning from ear to ear. She managed her small and large piece of luggage as she and Bruno enjoyed the familiar surroundings. It was one of the busiest train stations in Italy, an example of Italian modernism, built in 1934 during the Mussolini era. They walked through the sleek marble building and headed for the taxi stand.

On the way to the Grand Hotel Mediterraneo, the second hotel of their package, their driver, an attractive woman in her 30's, spoke in Italian about owning her own cab. She paid 400,000 euros for the license and made a good living, she said, especially during the summer months. She drove them to their huge and relatively new hotel. Their room was clean and simple; the bathroom offered the complimentary soap, shampoo, and conditioner that distinguished a four star from a three star hotel.

After checking email they walked north to the Piazza Cesare Beccaria. The circular piazza was full of traffic. They found a modern café and stopped for a sandwich in the uninteresting neighborhood. The deli was small and informal, just what they were looking for. The next day they would be up early to eat the hotel's breakfast and, this time, feel more rested, Bridget would join the 9 a.m. walking tour.

They awoke to a chilly overcast day. Their tour group took a long walk to some of the major piazzas of Florence: Piazza del Duomo, Piazza della Signoria, and Piazza della Repubblica, and to Palazzo Vecchio. Their tour guide's name was RRRRoberto (he made them practice rolling their R's). He was scholarly and interesting, adding stories of meeting his American wife many years ago when she was leading tours in Florence. The group finished at Piazza del Duomo and the East Bapistry doors. RRRRoberto made them laugh when he told them of giving his in-laws from Nebraska a similar tour. He had pointed out to his mother-in-law that it took Lorenzo Ghiberti fifty years to complete the famous bronze panels. He imitated her slow-drawl, broad-plains accent, sharing her comment, "How 'bout that." Roberto's story, and the doors, were memorable.

Afterwards, Bridget and Bruno wasted no time in setting out on their own. It was a cool morning and they decided to ride the C1, C2, C3, and C4 city mini-buses for what was left of the day to refresh their memories and get their bearings. Bruno always was prepared with ample bus tickets which he purchased in the *tabacchi*. They would use these buses often when, after three nights in Rome and the completion of the Gate 1 itinerary, they would be back to stay for a month in Florence in an apartment in the San Frediano neighborhood. Bridget's heart fluttered as they walked across the Ponte Santa Trinità on their way to locate their apartment. It was not far from Piazza Santo Spirito.

Walking in San Frediano, they noticed a trattoria at the end of the block. Bridget thought it looked like their kind of place for a splurge, especially since they had been very modest in their dining so far. It was 1 p.m., so many locals were inside enjoying the leisurely lunch break.

Bridget and Bruno ordered pasta, salads, bubbly water and a bottle of wine. They sat in a cozy back room, enjoying the classic cuisine. They finished with an espresso. The bill was a bit too high, so it was the last time there for them. Later that day, when they were walking in Piazza Santo Spirito, they stopped in their familiar Bar Ricchi for panini and wine at prices more to their liking.

In the morning they were up and out early to take a high-speed train to Rome. Bridget and Bruno usually booked economy seats, but their Gate 1 deal included premium tickets. They both enjoyed the perks—a large clean bathroom, plenty of luggage space, wi-fi access, and complimentary snacks. In no time they were in Rome.

ROME

The couple's information from Gate 1 said that the hotel was near the Termini train station. The entire tour group rolled their luggage a short distance to the Venetia Palace Hotel and squeezed into the small lobby to get room assignments. Bruno and Bridget lucked out, getting a room in a new addition across the interior courtyard. Their bathroom was luxurious. Fellow travelers shared stories of narrow shower stalls that prohibited bending down if a bar of soap was dropped.

Bridget wanted to stay in the room and rest as much as Bruno wanted to dash out and explore. He had heard about a fancy food court at the Termini station and in the neighborhood there were museums that he had read about. He would pick up dinner at the nearby supermarket and they would picnic in the courtyard, using one of the dozen available bistro tables. It was a temperate March evening by the time they settled into their meal of bread, cheese, wine, roasted vegetables and chicken.

They were up early the next morning for the complimentary breakfast. In all three hotels, bacon and scrambled eggs were served in large chafing dishes. In each case, the bacon was barely cooked and the eggs were also wet and sloppy. Otherwise, the food selection was agreeable. There were meats, cheeses, pastries, yogurt, cereal, toast and, most important, cappuccino.

Bridget and Bruno went by subway to join the group at the Vatican Museum for a 9 a.m. guided tour. They spent time in the Vatican gardens before being whisked through the museum halls, laden with art, to the Sistine Chapel. They were allowed 10 minutes to view the details and Michelangelo's frescoed ceiling with scenes from Genesis. A tour of St. Peter's Cathedral followed. It was sumptuous and marble clad. Bridget liked the generous decoration of golden *putti* (cherubs) of differing sizes.

The group had to keep to a tight schedule because the Chinese President, Xi Jinping, would arrive at noon as the guest of the Vatican. Black limousines were already arriving, and hundreds of chairs were set up outside for the ceremonies.

After the tour, Bruno and Bridget stopped nearby for some pizza and went to a large grocery store to pick up picnic items from the deli section. It would be a perfect night for another meal in the hotel courtyard. Bridget would have loved to spend a day on the hop-on hop-off bus, touring the major monuments as they had done once before. Unlike Bruno, she was taking her immersion into Italian life slowly while he was off and running.

After another generous breakfast the following morning, Bruno went to the Capitoline Museum and Bridget stayed behind to take advantage of the hotel spa. The set-up was disappointing. The steam room was shut down for repair. After three rounds of sauna and cool shower sequences, Bridget went back to the room to wait for Bruno. Luckily she had a good book. When Bruno returned they set off for the Palazzo Massimo alle Terme, an easy walk from the hotel. They spent several hours in the Renaissance-style palace, built in 1883-1887. It housed ancient Roman art: paintings, sculptures, mosaics, and jewelry, and was just the right size for Bridget. She got overwhelmed in large museums and only enjoyed a few rooms where objects where not crammed together. Outside they heard crowds gathering for a protest, which they learned happened every weekend for one cause or another.

That evening they dressed up (Bridget adding a scarf and Bruno a tie) and went to dinner in the neighborhood with a couple they had met on the tour. It was fun to get to know some fellow travelers. Mindy and Mike would be returning to their home in Florida the next day. The younger couple had optioned for additional tours and a cooking class to their trip. Bridget and Bruno never liked to pack too many events into one day.

The restaurant meal was a disappointment, but the company was delightful. Bridget's eyes bugged out when she ordered a Caesar salad and they brought greens with a small side dish of sour cream for the dressing! Their new friends had mentioned the salad as a selling point. Bridget should have known the restaurant was catering to tourists. She assuaged her disappointment by telling herself they had plenty of good eating ahead; she was truly looking forward to their month in Florence.

Spring in Florence

Bruno and Bridget had a special lilt in their step when they got out of the cab they had taken from Florence's Santa Maria Novella Station. A gentle breeze greeted them and they had arrived right on time to meet their rental agent, Alessandra. Bridget was prepared to scale the forty steps up to their Vacation Rental by Owner (VRBO) apartment—she had been practicing climbing the stairs in their condo back home. However, she was grateful that for the next month she would not have to repeat this climb with two heavy suitcases.

The apartment was just as it had been pictured in the listing. There was a large main room with a classic wooden dining table and five chairs, and a living room area with a TV, couch, and two barrel chairs which Bruno and Bridget came to like. In the living room a large antique credenza held all the kitchen items—pots, dishes, and flatware. Above the credenza hung a giant mirror in a gold frame.

There were two windows in the smaller bedroom and two in the living room, both facing the formidable bell tower of the magnificent church of San Frediano, built between 1680-1689 by the Roman architect Giulia Cervitti. The bell tower was completed in 1698 by Antonio Ferri.

The kitchen area was against the opposite wall. It was an open floor plan and it was pleasing and similar to their set-up at home. They had a washing machine and a dishwasher.

Bruno paid special attention to the quick rundown Alessandra gave of how to operate the appliances. Bridget asked about places where locals liked to eat in the neighborhood, mentioning how much they enjoyed Casalinga off Piazza Santo Spirito because of its classic Italian menu with reasonable prices.

"If you like Casalinga, you will like Sabatino's just on the other side of the ancient wall," Alessandra said as she rationed out the linens and towels for them and their guests. She informed them that the heat would turn on automatically when the room was a certain temperature and that when they left they should just leave the keys on the table. Then she was out the door. All of that took fifteen minutes.

Bridget felt like she was playing house. She and Bruno unpacked and moved clothing into two large armoires in the ample bedroom with a half-bath en suite. The room, in the back of the apartment, had ladder-like stairs against the wall leading to a loft sleeping area. This was hardly more than a wooden canopy with a single bed and writing desk and chair. Bridget couldn't stand up straight as she climbed to the loft and not easily once she was up there. Every movement could be heard as it echoed. Nobody ended up using it. Bridget was grateful that they hadn't needed to.

The small second bedroom had twin beds and an armoire. The apartment was attractive and Bridget could feel that it was put together with love and an elegance now worn at the edges. She welcomed the opportunity to soak up Florence once again, with its beauty at every turn. This they would share with guests as spring came into bloom.

They would be joined by friends who would use the second bedroom for three weeks of their month-long stay. First would come Christine and Luigi from Treviglio for a night, then Sallie for two weeks and their friend Tammy for six nights. Sallie had spent a week with them in Florence fifteen years ago. This would be Tammy's first visit to Italy, the home of her great grandparents.

Bruno and Bridget were ready to explore the neighborhood and fill their larder with some groceries. They would need coffee and cream for the morning, something for dinner, and wine. All of this and more they found at the COIN (a chain throughout Italy) grocery a few blocks away, just off Piazza San Carmine. After returning and putting their groceries away they headed for Piazza Santo Spirito and ordered a spritz and panini at Bar Ricchi. On the five-block walk there, they noticed many small businesses (a tailor, an eyeglass frame shop, small cafés) and places to eat ranging from fancy to simple. It was exciting to be in a new neighborhood and yet be close to familiar places like those in Santo Spirito.

During the early part of their trip they had firmed up plans, through email, to meet a friend from Eugene, Bill Allord, a mosaic artist. To celebrate his 70th birthday, he was spending 70 days in Italy. They were to meet in front of the famous baptistry doors across from the Duomo at 11 a.m. the next day.

They awoke to a cool grey morning, much like they were used to in Eugene. With two bathrooms, Bridget and Bruno had an easy time getting ready. The larger had a walk-in shower. After numerous pots of espresso from the cafetteria, half the size of theirs at home, and some bread and berries, they headed toward their meeting, crossing the Arno on Ponte Santa Trinità. Bridget felt excitement as she looked down at the water. There was a single kayak on the river. The water reflected the grey sky. Onward past the fancy shop windows they went, stopping at a familiar café for an espresso so that Bridget could use the bathroom. Many people stood at the bar for a quick caffè and treat. The glass shelves of pastries were so inviting they couldn't resist: Bruno ordered a sweet and Bridget a savory.

Bruno and Bridget were known for being punctual, and they met Bill exactly on time. They admired the bronze doors of the Baptistry as they had with their guide, RRRRoberto, on the walking tour a few days earlier. They walked around the Duomo, admiring the magnificence of the exterior. Back in Eugene, they often visited with Bill at craft fairs where he sold mosaic photo frames and other items. This trip, he was traveling solo. He had visited Italy several times before and insisted they try one of his favorite places to eat while in Florence, the trattoria *da Mario*. He couldn't believe they had never been there! They set off toward Mercato Centrale in Piazza San Lorenzo. Mario's was nearby, and a favorite of the workers at the mercato. Apparently it was many people's favorite — they had to wait outside for their name to come up on the list. When called, they squeezed into a space and sat at a long shared table. Bridget thought that getting in looked undoable, but all of the happy faces of satisfied customers made the impossible possible.

Bill, a good-looking and warm fellow, was known at Mario's. When in Florence, he was a repeat guest. He received much both-cheek-kissing and hugging from the owner and the staff. His secret, he said, was to keep an address book, writing down the names of everyone he met when he traveled.

After the three gave their order for grilled chicken, pasta pomodoro, a simple green salad and wine, a woman who was so striking that she turned every head came and sat next to Bill. They assumed she was Italian. She was a statuesque brunette, with long hair, olive complexion, and dark eyes. However, she told them her name was Julia, a stewardess with United Airlines from New Jersey. She had come to eat at Mario's on a friend's recommendation. As they chatted, Bridget found herself slipping into the mother role since Julia was around the age of her daughter Sarina. When the young Italian man to Bridget's right offered to pay for the young stewardess' wine and lunch, she accepted, but was careful to walk out of Mario's with Bridget, Bruno, and Bill. By the time they reached the Duomo, Julia was ready to set off on her own. Bridget thought she heard Bill sigh as the young woman walked away. Bill, Bridget and Bruno headed off for gelato. Mario's was a true find.

Later that evening, Bruno joined Bill at the Odeon Cinema to watch a movie about Paul Gauguin. Bridget stayed at the apartment and read, but hoped to eventually catch a movie in the Odeon as they had done in earlier stays. She preferred a matinee. The Odeon's interior was built in the style of the Renaissance treasure, Palazzo Stro-zzino, which was designed by Philippo Brunelleschi, who had also designed the dome of the Duomo and the basilica, Santo Spirito. It was a comfortable theatre that frequently showed English movies.

Two days later they heard from Bill. He had been robbed in Gaeta, a small town between Rome and Naples. All of his credit cards and euros were gone. He still had his passport and rental car, but reported being in dire straits. What could they do to help? They quickly sent back some suggestions and the offer to stay in their loft for a night if he needed to come to Florence.

The police in Gaeta found him a safe place to sleep that first night. In a day, his wallet turned up with all of the credit cards intact and only the euros missing. He was off on his adventure once again. Bridget and Bruno were relieved, and they took extra care with their credit cards and euros, knowing this calamity could happen to anyone.

Sabatino's

After a slow, relaxing morning catching up on emails in the apartment, Bridget and Bruno walked across Ponte Santa Trinità to the Duomo and Baptistry where, through his research, Bruno had located a small free museum nearby. The Misericordia di Firenze was only open for ten minutes, at 10 a.m. and again at 12 noon. They were the only visitors in the two rooms of the late gothic Loggia del Bigalla, which held twenty paintings and some artifacts. They were both pleased with Bruno's discovery. This was just the sort of adventure Bridget could count on him uncovering. As they were leaving, a group of twenty lively grade school aged children on a field trip with two teachers arrived, only to be told to come back at noon.

In their further exploration by city bus, Bridget and Bruno located the Mercato Sant'Ambrogio. Bruno had visited before, but not Bridget. The Sant'Ambrogio market was a smaller version of the Mercato Centrale, about a fourth of the size. There they found everything they could need that was fresh and also special enough for Christine and Luigi, who would arrive in three days. Being Italian, Luigi was a lover of the best and the freshest food of the region. That is what they had been treated to at their wedding two years ago. They purchased goat and sheep cheese, prosciutto, lettuce, tomatoes, bread, ragu and fresh pasta. Most would soon be eaten but there would be cheese saved for a small plate with a glass of wine to welcome Christine and Luigi. The sights and smells in the mercato made Bridget hungry.

At home they put their food away and then walked a few blocks just outside the medieval gate of San Frediano. Their destination for lunch was Trattoria Sabatino. They found it to be a wonderful family restaurant. Bridget had read in the guidebook that it "hasn't been tarted up like many of the older restaurants in Florence." They also remembered their VRBO agent had recommended it enthusiastically as well.

Inside the restaurant's open room there were many tables for eight. The dining room was large by Florence standards. Small antiques were perched on high shelving circling the room. Windows let in ample light, lending the room a warm brown tone. The décor could have been the same for the last eighty years. They chatted for a moment with a couple of travelers from France who joined Bridget and Bruno at their table.

The food was good and the prices unbelievable. Pastas cost 4,20 euros, vegetable side dishes and salads 2,70 euros. Each guest had one small glass which was to be used for water or wine. Bridget memorized the menu, knowing they would be back with friends. The staff worked with preci- sion and harmony. It was family owned and operated. The grey-haired Mamma was definitely orchestrating the crew. Everything was simply prepared from fresh regional ingre- dients, the classic way of Italian cooking.

As they were paying at the cashier's counter, Bridget noticed, off to the side, a local newspaper clipping. She rec- ognized the staff of Sabatino's with Anthony Bourdain and his sweetheart, the actress and film director Asia Argento. The photo was taken in 2018, one month before his death. It took Bridget's breath away. In the photo the group was cutting up for the camera, with their arms across each other's shoulders like a chorus line.

Anthony's work documented international culture, cuisine, and the human condition. News of his suicide had shaken Bridget. She had not known of his history of depression until after his death. It hit her hard for all of the people who were also struggling, so she felt more vulnerable and shaken. Bourdain's love of the simple and good food of working men and women was what Bridget focused on when she cooked or traveled. He was a very good writer. Bridget's answer to "Who would you like to have lunch with, if it could be anyone?" would be Anthony Bourdain.

As they walked the few blocks home, the church bells of San Frediano rang. She said a prayer. She found herself, when visiting Italy, more prone to wrap herself in faith. They went into at least one church every day. Bruno studied the art and the architecture and she lit candles and sat in the pews and prayed. As they walked she took Bruno's hand and drew closer to him.

Even in Eugene she was spending more time in her church, Saint Mary's Episcopal, finding peace there. The two hours a week that she spent volunteering at the welcome desk centered her. The way that clergy and staff walked in faith was a model for her. She knew she needed more work to consistently be her best-self. In Italy, she was surrounded by the history of churches centuries old.

Company

Christine and Luigi would have only one night in Florence so they wanted it to be a memorable one. Bruno had cased the neighborhood and beyond for the freshest morning pastries; Bridget shopped for the best meats and cheeses of Tuscany. Bridget had known Christine all of her life. Bruno had known Patricia, Christine's mother, since she was a girl, half a century ago.

They had all been together the previous summer when the young couple visited Eugene. The newlyweds had come to Oregon to exchange wedding vows and celebrate with friends and family who were stateside and hadn't witnessed their Italian wedding. The celebration took place in the backyard of Christine's childhood home, which had been recently transformed by her parents, Patricia and George, and a landscape designer. The event was a distillation of the joy and connection of their Italian celebration. The ceremony was different, seasoned with a year of marriage. The newlyweds were more casually dressed. Christine wore a white crepe jumpsuit that tied around the neck revealing a bared back. Luigi wore a more casual shirt without a tie. Their friend, Angela, led the ceremony. The couple entered the garden and faced each other. The words exchanged reflected the maturity they had gained over the past year, learning to work together and work things out. Bridget and Bruno were subdued at this event, grateful to be taking it all in.

A buffet of Mexican food and wedding beverages was served and once again there was dancing into the warm summer night. Strings of twinkling lights had been set up in a profusion of visual impact. Relatives came from across the country and Italy. Close friends were ready to celebrate the union. The couple's entire visit lasted several weeks and Bridget and Bruno spent several warm summer evenings with them.

Almost a year later, in Florence, on the crisp morning of the last Saturday in March, Christine and Luigi arrived from Treviglio, traveling light. They walked from the train station. A day later they would be traveling home.

Bridget looked out the window of their apartment just as Christine and Luigi were coming down the sidewalk across the street. "Buongiorno!" she called out in her teacher voice, which easily carried four floors below. Christina looked up with her radiant smile.

Greetings, hugs and kisses were exchanged as soon as the couple came inside. Christine was newly wearing glasses, which added an element of seriousness to her personal style. Luigi was full of his youthful energy. He was handsome, not unusual for men in Italy. To this Luigi brought warmth and charm. Bridget had met his father at the wedding in Treviglio, so it was clear to her where Luigi's warmth came from. Bridget and Bruno's hair grew whiter and whiter as each year passed. Yet when Bridget looked at this young couple, she felt young again.

The plan was to have a snack and then walk to the Mercato Centrale. Two streets bordering the mercato are lined with vendors. Christine wanted to return to the outside stall of the merchant from whom she had purchased a leather purse the year before. She intended to get the same purse in a more useful color, perhaps a darker blue.

Having a full-time teaching job, Christine had been able to purchase a car in the last year. She described the challenge of acquiring an Italian license. There was a very thick book to master, which included how the parts of the car worked. Luigi was working in marketing in Bergamo.

As the two couples crossed Ponte Santa Trinità, they laughed and snapped pictures. Christine and Luigi made Bridget and Bruno promise not to tell anyone—they planned to move to Eugene, hopefully by the next Christmas. Christine had been living in Italy for seven years. She missed her family, friends and their new niece, the infant daughter of her oldest sister Ellen. The news of their pending move brightened the day even more for Bridget.

The purchase of the purse went smoothly. Afterwards they stopped in Santo Spirito for aperitivi. This put everyone in the mood for a short nap before their planned 8:00 p.m. dinner.

Luigi had made reservations at Diladdarno, away from the tourist areas and very close to the apartment. The small trattoria boasted mind-boggling good food, homemade and typical of Tuscany. The bond between the servers, who were family, was charming. Diladdarno had been in the family for over 100 years! Bruno and Bridget enjoyed sformato as their primi. They had never experienced this savory, vegetable flan before. Christine and Luigi told them it was served year-round and yet, somehow, they had missed it! The entire dinner was a tasty feast of authentic Florentine cooking.

The couples retired early. The next morning they were up for espresso and pastries, then they walked together to a small free museum that Bruno had discovered in his reading. Bridget had to remind them to slow down. Her aches and pains made it hard to keep up, especially without a slow warmup.

The exhibit was in a palazzo facing the Arno and was called, colloquially, the 007 Museum. It had been the home of Rodolfo Siviero, who recovered a great number of pieces of Italian art that had been looted during World War II. Siviero was a dashing man and very popular with the ladies, hence the nickname. Visitors are allowed into the ground floor rooms of the 19th century home to see Rodolfo's personal collection of art.

The young couple were eager to introduce Bruno and Bridget to Osteria All'Antico Vinaio for lunch. Although the sandwich hole-in-the-wall had existed in Florence for decades, Bruno and Bridget had missed it. They were warned not to be deterred by the line winding around the block in the center of Florence, not far from the Uffizi Gallery.

Waiting in line, Christine and Luigi talked about how magical it would be to recreate the eatery in Eugene. The osteria offered popular 5 euro sandwiches on a crusty homemade flat bread (like focaccia, sliced for a top and bottom) featuring combos of cured meats, cheese and vegetable spreads that were of the finest Tuscan quality. The line moved fast and they were soon leaving with four take-away sandwiches, plastic cups, and a bottle of red wine. The couples wandered to the edge of the crowd and found a window ledge for their cups as they enjoyed their stand-up picnic. Previously, Bridget had always thought it was a sacred rule never to put more than two ingredients in a panino. Her mind had now been changed.

    Virginia Salinsky Landgreen

They headed back to the apartment to say their good-byes. Bridget felt wistful as she watched Christine and Luigi stroll to the station. They left a bit early so that they could linger in the romantic streets and markets of bella Firenze.

Amici

The day after Christine and Luigi left, Sallie arrived from her home in Jupiter, Florida. Again Bridget leaned out the antiquated wooden window just as Sallie stepped out of the taxi. Her tinkling laughter lifted on the air and Bridget greeted her with a "Buongiorno!" from the fourth floor. Sallie looked up and waved, happy to have completed her traveling and to begin her two weeks in Florence.

Bridget helped Sallie carry her suitcase and travel pack up the forty steps to the apartment. Once inside they hugged and giggled with joy to be together in Italy. Sallie always looked stylish and smart and the long flight had hardly ruffled her.

Bruno soon returned from shopping and served some prosecco, cheese and fruit. The three chatted and caught up on recent events and plans. There would be a gelato festival at Piazzale Michelangelo, and several large art shows in palazzi that Bridget and Bruno thought Sallie would enjoy.

They had tickets for a wine tour that included visits to other Tuscan cities. Sallie had come with recommendations for fine dining from colleagues. She still had a few clients from her marketing career, though she was mostly retired. She had achieved financial success from her career in advertising and gained a high level of sophistication from dealing with clients like Ford, Warner Bros. and Hallmark. She had been one of the first women to take a place at the table within the patriarchy of 1970's advertising, yet she remained grounded. Sallie was a super pal to both Bruno and Bridget. The three friends had shared many adventures over the last decades.

In the past two years, Bridget had experienced more than her usual anxiety for a number of reasons. Her life and her family seemed to have more challenges. She was horrified at the losses to health and human services that the GOP was targeting. Eugene recently counted 1,600 homeless people.

She had told Sallie before the trip that she might have to hold her hand. It had been a wonderful diversion for her to plan the trip, but it was also not a good time for Bruno to leave a backlog of work and bills for five weeks. Bridget had her own list of reasons for not wanting to go. Each day she meditated and medicated to help her anxiety.

Finishing their snack, Bruno and Bridget gave Sallie an orientation to the apartment and its quirks. She could use the bigger bathroom, as Bruno and Bridget kept their toiletries in the half-bath off their bedroom. All of the kitchen dishes and cooking equipment were stored in the antique buffet in the dining room area. Meal preparations and shopping would be shared endeavors.

Next they introduced her to their neighborhood and made their way to Santo Spirito. Sallie was a girlhood friend of Bridget's; they met in 7th grade. A table in the sun at the Cabiria café was a perfect place to people watch. Bruno was interested in their cocktail menu. Sallie decided she would try a pink lady (egg white, grenadine, cream and gin), which became her cocktail of choice for the remainder of the trip. Bruno and Bridget ordered Campari spritz, the typical aperitivo in the late afternoon. These drinks came with a small bowl of nuts. The first afternoon of the "sweetness of doing nothing" was launched!

The market's outdoor vegetable stalls were packing up when they arrived in the piazza, so they instead shopped at the corner Conad market for dinner and breakfast items. They would return many times to this neighborhood store, part of a chain that carried frozen food, wine, fresh produce, prepared pasta dishes and limited household items.

Bridget was eager to show Sallie the sunken recycling system on the street not far away. The arrangement made it easy to sort glass, paper, metal, and plastic. The four bins were low to the ground. When the trucks came to collect recycling, they extracted each container, largely under-ground, hydraulically, and added the contents to the bins on the truck bed with loud mechanical sounds.

That evening Bridget and Bruno prepared a green salad to go with roasted chicken from the market. There was a side dish of pasta, simply prepared with garlic, olive oil and par-migiano cheese. Ample wine set them up for the night's sleep.

It was a slow morning. Everyone woke up at different times. Bruno bounced out of bed early, as usual. Bridget tried to sleep in after being up for a few hours in the middle of the night. This was an unfortunate pattern for her lately. Sallie slept in until 10:00 after her long flight. Breakfast was yogurt, espresso, fruit and pastries.

The trio were dressed and out the door by noon. They headed to the center of town, across Ponte Santa Trinità on the path now familiar to Bridget and Bruno. Sallie was once again thrilled to see the Duomo in Piazza del Duomo.

The three hundred and seventy-five foot structure topped with a dome of red tiles had been taking the breath away of visitors for over 500 years. Sallie's enthusiasm for sights that were now familiar to Bridget and Bruno helped reinvigorate their appreciation for Florence's beauty.

Their destination for this day was the photography show, *Bowie by Sukita*, which had just opened at the Palazzo Medici Riccardi. It consisted of 60 large-format photos taken over a forty-year partnership between the rock legend and the master photographer. These mostly off-stage pictures were stunning and playful. Bowie's love of dressing in outlandish costumes and posing were obvious. The juxtaposition between the modern and the ancient artifacts in the palazzo delighted them.

After a few hours they continued to explore the nearby palazzi. As they headed home, they stopped for a few items for dinner and picked up some bottles of wine. Each day they checked their iPhones and marveled at the number of steps they had taken. Even though they walked the same route, Bridget's steps were always hundreds fewer. It didn't seem fair to her. Her legs felt the most leaden, she was sure!

Once home, they cozied in for the night. They didn't get many channels on the TV and none were in English. Bridget missed BBC News, which they often followed when they traveled. Bridget and Bruno had begun to watch a weeknight program, *Guess My Age*. The host spoke English only when he pronounced the phrase (with a heavy Italian accent) that was the show's name. The cash prizes were high and it seemed to be a popular show, given the number of times it appeared during the week.

The mystery participant whose age was to be guessed would not say a word except a stern "No" when the wrong guess was given. The pair of participants doing the guessing would be doled out clues. The subject, usually a senior citizen, would, for example, hold up their hands in front of their chest and turn them front to back, as the camera zoomed in. Next, the person of mystery might be asked to dance for five seconds to some music, or would be asked to take off their glasses for a close up. At each wrong guess, the cash prize would dwindle. In the times that Bridget and Bruno tuned in, only once was the age guessed correctly. Bridget found it, like most game shows, uninteresting but it did make her laugh every time the host said "Guess My Age" with a strong accent. She made so many mistakes in her efforts to speak Italian; she had a warm spot for non-English speakers.

Their apartment host had left a dozen DVD's. Most were Barbara Streisand movies and, over the course of the month, they watched: *The Owl and the Pussycat*, *The Way We Were*, *Funny Girl*, *The Prince of Tides*, and *Yentl*. Bridget enjoyed them all. Her favorite was *The Prince of Tides*.

Bruno loved the challenge of figuring out how Italian appliances worked. Bridget had no natural instincts for machines and would always look on Bruno getting the DVD player to function as a small miracle.

They each tracked the weather on their iPhones or the weather channel on the TV. The next day would be sunny. They planned to spend it revisiting the Boboli Gardens and the Pitti Palace. Bridget was happy to have Sallie visit. She hoped she would get a better night's sleep. Bruno had found some grappa in their travels. It didn't appeal to Sallie but Bridget and Bruno toasted the good day with a few sips before bed.

The morning of their visit to the Boboli Gardens and Pitti Palace began with a slap-dash breakfast and quick preparations to get out the door. They wanted to get there early to avoid the crowds. Once again Bridget had slept poorly, waking up and not being able to fall back to sleep. It was crisp and sunny as they walked through Santo Spirito to the Pitti Palace. They had planned to each buy one ticket for both places, but the options had changed since they had last been there: now two tickets would be required. They decided to explore the garden today and buy a ticket to the Pitti Palace another day. Even though they got an early start, the wait in the ticket line was forty-five minutes.

Once inside the grounds, Bridget, Bruno, and Sallie went directly to the small café at the edge of the courtyard. They sat down—something they rarely did because of the added cost—and enjoyed an assortment of small panini and capuccini. They had been rushing and standing and needed a rest. The elegant space was busy with people, mostly standing at the bar to take advantage of the 10:30 a.m. tradition of a little pick-me-up to stave off hunger until a later lunch.

Fortified to explore the 111-acre garden, they were led by Bruno up the tiny pebbled pathways. Laid out for the Medici family after they bought the Palazzo Pitti in 1549, the gardens are an excellent example of Renaissance landscaping. They stopped by the grottos on the way into the garden. These small artificial caves are picturesque and provide relief from heat in the summer.

They wended their way through the geometric patterns of arches and boxwood hedges to the top of the first section, then through the wilder groves of oak and cypress trees to the building that housed a porcelain collection. Bridget and Sallie were drawn to the china collections while Bruno admired the many art pieces.

Bridget had been all over the acreage in former visits to Florence and her heart wasn't up for more close observation on this day. She told herself to be happy for the exercise and good company. Since it was early April, few flowers were in bloom. Sallie had not seen the neighboring gardens of Villa Bardini, which had been closed for restoration during most of the last decade. The two gardens were very different. The huge Boboli laid out in 1549 and the small Bardini, designed in the late 1900s, were a nice complement to each other.

Bruno remembered the way into the Bardini, which almost adjoined the Boboli. They soon found themselves in a fifty-yard tunnel of tree limbs forming an overhead arching canopy. It was a super spot for photos, although almost anywhere they had paused in the last two hours of strolling would also have been excellent. The view from the highest point was comparable to that at Piazzale Michelangelo, minus the crowds. Not every tourist noticed that entry to both gardens was included with the ticket to the Boboli gardens, or maybe guests had walked all the miles that they could in the first magnificent garden. Countless beautiful statues lined the garden's steep inclines, and birdsong filled the air. The only other people in the Bardini garden were grounds crews with specialized, heavy duty lifts that they were using to prune the tall trees and hedges.

During the recent days, Bridget felt under a cloud. She knew herself enough to know that she was always homesick when she reached the three-week mark in a trip. She missed her children on both sides of the country and her granddaughter so much she ached. The pain was acute on Sarina's birthday. Bridget also missed her heartfelt talks with her sister, Anna. She tried to consider this when planning, but she couldn't resist the discount for renting their apartment for a month. When would she learn, she thought glumly, as they were walking away from the gardens? Bruno was just settling into his traveling high-gear at the time Bridget was waning.

They planned an event each day. These were perhaps more satisfying to Bridget as she looked back on them once they were home. She missed the stamina and walking speed that she used to possess when they first started their Italian adventures decades ago. She chose comfort over style in her black slip-on men's walking shoes. They helped because they had great support and an extra thick sole for the varying terrain. On their first Italian trip her shoes pinched and never felt solid on uneven surfaces. She had adopted ugly shoes for every trip that followed. At this point in her life, sensible shoes always won out over stylish ones.

They walked down the hill to re-enter the town for lunch. This time they picked a table under an umbrella at Buca dell'Orafo (loosely, the cubbyhole of the goldsmiths) and ordered a big meal. Bridget's spirits picked up immediately. The sun was shining, the company grand. Soon they gave themselves over to large plates of homemade pasta and a carafe of house wine!

Over the next week they visited the bustling Mercato Centrale, enjoying the new food court on the second floor. There were families with young children and grandparents sharing lunch at long tables in the center surrounded by many stations offering meals at a fixed rate. They each ordered a hearty roast chicken and potato lunch. Later in the week they returned for the famous boiled beef sandwich with a plastic cup of wine from da Nerbone, which had been serving crowds since 1872.

Another day they revisited The Officina Profumo Farmaceutica di Santa Maria Novella. Credited with being the oldest pharmacy in the world, the luxurious interior of the store was beyond any Bridget had ever seen. It looked like a cathedral to her: golden walls and fixtures, chandeliers, and stained glass. Sallie was happy to return to this shopping experience. She remembered it well from her visit in 2003.

While Bridget was usually more of a bargain shopper, she believed these scented lotions, ancient preparations, and perfumes were heavenly and medicinal. Knowing that she could now order online (orders over 200 euros shipped free from Italy), she left without any purchases. With items averaging 100 euros, it wasn't hard to fill an order back home. She still had cologne and perfume purchased in 2001, proving a little bit of luxury goes a long way.

The next day they visited the Ferragamo Shoe Museum. This modern exhibit displayed photographs, patents, sketches, and even wooden lasts made for Marilyn Monroe and various other famous feet of the stars. Both shoes and clothing were featured. The current exhibit was *Sustainable Thinking* and was about fashion and ecology. Bridget particularly enjoyed the permanent collection of shoe styles through the ages in this gallery setting in the basement of a former medieval palace.

Later that day they found the small gallery, Faustini Arte, at the Borgo Ognissanti address where Sallie's friend in the U.S. had purchased a piece of art on his honeymoon the year before. That gallery was a delight. The artist, Uliviero Ulivieri, a contemporary Florence native, had a show full of whimsy and charm. The series featured stick-like figures of nuns and priests frolicking in piazzas, on rooftops, at the beach, and on ice. There often were as many as twenty habit-clad clergy showing a contagious fun spirit. These delightful finds distracted Bridget from being homesick.

On the rainy Sunday in the middle of Sallie's stay they dressed warmly and visited Florence's second-ranked (after the Uffizi) museum, the Bargello. This was Bridget's favorite. There were three floors and many rooms, including a medley of Italy's finest Renaissance sculpture. Bridget remembered that, in 2001, Jaan could hardly wait to show her Donatello's David on the second floor. Nothing like the powerful David by Michelangelo that towered in the Accademia Gallery, this younger, boyish version was demure.

The Bargello had originally been the town hall. It was the oldest public building in Florence. From the courtyard on the ground floor to the top floor, the collection offered a grand experience.

Afterwards they ducked into a warm restaurant on Piazza Santo Spirito for drinks and dishes of pasta in a simple white sauce with asparagus. The outside got a good drenching while they ate. Rain pounded against the large, steamed-up windows.

On a sunny day they took a longer bus ride up to San Miniato al Monte, overlooking Piazzale Michelangelo. This large Romanesque church built over the shrine of San Miniato (St. Minias) required a climb of 200 steps. Bridget remembered it well because she and Bruno visited it three times during their month in Florence. Each time she would brace herself with a deep sigh and ascend!

Later they sampled their fill of gelato at the *Gelato Festival 2019*, the most prestigious individual gelato tournament in the world, held in the Piazzale Michelangelo. Sallie was the first to quit tasting. Bruno lasted the longest, sampling twenty small cups of different flavors. The flavors were novel: licorice, maple with bacon bits, and cherry with Amaretto, for example. One of the goals of the festival was to launch new flavors.

For an adventure out of town, they took the train to Prato (another rainy day) and visited the Museo del Tessuto, which traces the history of Italy's textile industry. The modern museum had first-rate exhibits. They learned that during World War ll fabric was decomposed into a new material for clothing. Nothing was wasted. There also were garments designed for the church or the nobility that were so fine they would qualify as works of art.

Their biggest adventure was a day-long bus tour with twenty other people to Siena, San Gimignano, and Monteriggioni that included lunch at the Famigla Mazzarini Vineyard. The meal did not disappoint and it was paired with wines that are never exported and only available for purchase onsite. This was a fast-paced tour. In Siena, Bridget and Sallie lost Bruno. The three of them had been enjoying the most enjoyable glass of Brunello Di Montalcino while sitting at a fancy trattoria on the shell-shaped main square, Piazza del Campo. Bruno's splurge for them was made more memorable by the formally clad waiter who ceremoniously rinsed the glasses with the wine, pouring a taste for Bruno to determine that the wine was not "off," and then instructing them, after pouring each a glass, that it was best if they sat with it for fifteen minutes before sipping. They obeyed and wondered if the wait made the wine more tasty. They relaxed and enjoyed being at the site of the lawless, bareback, medieval-style horse race which was held in the summer amid famous pageantry and civic identity.

Just a few seconds after they had savored the last drop of their wine, Bruno disappeared to pay the check, knowing that they needed to hurry to meet up with the group. But Bridget thought he had left through one of the crowded streets leading away from the famous outdoor piazza.

   Virginia Salinsky Landgreen

Maybe she was a little dazed from the wine? She had a moment of freak-out. In a panic she and Sallie raced up the nearest street. Realizing that they did not know what they were doing, they stopped.

Bridget managed to get directions to their gathering spot from a man who was standing by, talking with a friend, only after some wild-eyed, very broken Italian and frenzied hand motions. All of her life she had recurring nightmares about being lost. Luckily, on this day, they found Bruno and joined the group. They were soon whisked back to the outlying area where the buses were parked. The tour guide's fast walking pace was the sort of thing that put Bridget in a foul mood. She realized she had become spoiled by her personal tour guide, Bruno, even though she didn't always appreciate it.

For Bridget, one of the most memorable locations they visited during Sallie's Florence visit was the Synagogue and Jewish Museum on Borgo la Croce. In all of their previous trips they had missed what to Bridget was one of the most beautiful and meaningful places of worship she had ever visited. Bruno positioned a yarmulke on his head and the trio spent a long time in the sacred space, one of the largest synagogues (Tempio Maggiore) in south-central Europe. It was built between 1874–1882. The Jewish people of Florence have one of the oldest continuous communities in Europe.

The colors and intricacies of the small designs covering every inch of the huge place of worship were stunning. The patterns were in shades of turquoise, blue, gold, red and burnt orange. The Temple, made of travertine and pink pomato stone in the Moorish style, had a golden light filtering through its windows. The architects, Marco Treves, Mariano Falcini, and Vincenzo Micheli, placed the dome between two towers.

Upstairs, the women's gallery had wrought-iron railings adorned with seven-branch candelabras.

In a case in the next room that also contained religious objects, documents told the history of the Florentine Jewish community. The upstairs exhibit covered the cruelty and decimation of the Jewish population during World War ll. Bridget's awareness of these atrocities had started, as for many pre-teens, with the reading of *The Diary of Anne Frank*. Man's inhumanity to man weighed on her young years. She and Sallie had read the book in junior high school. Bridget remembered Sallie (like Bridget, a Lutheran) wearing a Star of David around her neck through high school. The weight of Jewish history was felt again during the presidency of Donald Trump. Hate crimes were increasing in America.

Oppression, cruelty, and exploitation of other cultures were not new. What happened to the Jewish population was one of history's worst horrors. Bridget read that during most of the 300 years of Medici times, the Jewish population had to remain within the locked gates of their separate living area from sun-down to sun-up. This information, new to her, further shattered her belief that mankind was capable of world peace.

Bruno had another memorable experience when he went into the men's bathroom and one of the armed guards who had been stationed at the entrance was using the urinal next to him. The guard's machine gun kept banging on the porcelain.

Bridget regretted that in 2001, when Sarina and her best friend Joanna were staying with them in Florence, Bridget had missed the opportunity to visit the Synagogue and Museum with Jo, who went all by herself to explore her Jewish heritage. That evening Jo was quieter than usual.

Wrapping It Up with a Holiday Bow

By the end of Sallie's visit they had shared glorious meals at Trattoria Giovanni, Pandemonio, and Sabatino's. The first two were Sallie's treat based on suggestions from her friends. Bruno loved Pandemonio, Sallie's favorite was Giovanni's, and Bridget's tastes were loyal to Sabatino's. They prepared meals in the apartment as well, feeling clever because they managed in the kitchen with its limited utensils.

Often in the mornings the three would start at the dining table with coffee, fresh berries and Greek yogurt. Then out came their laptops, as they each appreciated news from home. Most days had an easy rhythm. Sallie was light hearted and confident. She had a good-sized travel budget. This trip was one of several international journeys for her in 2019. She had many more social circles than Bridget and Bruno who loved alone time or each other's company. If they were lucky they could visit Italy every other year.

On Sallie's last morning they woke up early, said their Italian-drenched goodbyes, and helped Sallie and her two pieces of luggage into a cab to the Florence airport. They knew they would be seeing her again in six months when she came to Oregon, which kept this parting from being too sad. Bridget immediately got busy changing linens and preparing for their final guest. She smiled as she did these chores, anticipating the outlook of the younger guest from Oregon.

Later that day Tammy Paladini arrived from Rome. Bruno walked to the station to meet her and they took a cab back to the apartment. She had managed all of the travel changes and challenges with a huge backpack half her size. They figured she must be exhausted but she claimed that she wasn't. To say that Tammy's joy to be in Italy was infectious was an understatement. Two previous years she had bought tickets but then cancelled, first because she was ill and then because her cat Olive was sick.

Tammy was Sarina and John's friend of many years. That's how Bridget and Bruno got to know this Portland artist and volunteer coordinator for hospice. Bridget and Sarina had purchased several of her paintings over the years. Tammy had performed so much Reiki on Sarina recently that it felt like part of Bridget's daughter was with them in the spirit of their guest. Reiki is a healing technique based on the principle that energy can be channeled into the patient by means of touch. Tammy began her Reiki training to help her cat, Olive, in her declining years.

They welcomed Tammy with a short walk to Piazza Santo Spirito. Their first stop was the basilica, then they stepped outside to watch life in the piazza from an umbrella table with a glass of wine and some snacks. The weather was warming in this last week of April. The short stroll home along the Arno was just enough to orient Tammy before a dinner in the apartment of salad greens, pasta with meat sauce, wonderful cheese and wine. It wasn't long before she was ready to call it a day (actually, two!).

In the six nights that the three spent together, they walked and bused to major sites, climbing the 200 steps to San Miniato and also enjoying Piazzale Michelangelo's panoramic view.

They returned to Piazza Santo Spirito and popped into artist studios in the neighborhood. The Oltrarno area has remained a home for artisans. Bruno translated and Tammy chatted with Italians in both studios they visited. In one, the gentleman restored antique furniture and in the other a father and daughter were painters.

Tammy had scheduled two private art classes for her Florence visit. Bruno had a great sense of purpose accompanying her to the locations, seeing her off like a proud parent. Her dark eyes, angelic smile, and beautiful face, crowned with brunette curls, were so ready for Italy. She would begin the day with wet hair from the shower, a scrubbed face and red lipstick. Tammy returned from class the first day with two oil paintings of considerable size. Bridget was sure that Tammy's feet never touched the ground between the school and the apartment!

The larger of the paintings was a study of a nude male in a classic pose. The smaller, which she presented to Bridget and Bruno as a gift, was the head of Michelangelo's David with an insert of a young woman with a large white dog at her side. Both paintings were incredible, in Bridget's opinion.

Tammy had reservations to visit the Accademia and the Uffizi Galleries. She was an independent house guest, easy to be with. The three enjoyed sitting in the soft light of the apartment in the evenings, retracing the day and basking in Tammy's discoveries.

During this time Bruno and Bridget enjoyed opportunities to wander in the city or have some alone time as the date of their departure drew closer.

While Tammy was in Florence they shared meals at Sabatino's and other neighborhood spots that Bruno and Bridget knew were good. One afternoon they all met Tammy after her class and had lunch at the Gran Caffè San Marco, where case after case was filled with Easter confections. Tammy would be taking the train to join a friend in Assisi the Saturday before Easter, then visit Rome and other cities in Italy. Bruno and Bridget knew from experience that being in Assisi for Easter was near perfection although they would not be going this time. Tammy had been waiting for this trip for nearly a decade and she was psyched to make the most of it, pushing herself to be as extroverted as her quiet nature could allow.

It dawned on Bridget that most restaurants in Italy would be closed on Easter Sunday and Holy Monday. She wanted to take the short train ride to the seaside resort town of Viareggio, known for its pre-lenten carnival. Her fond memories of the day they spent there in 2001 were calling her. The allegorical figures that were part of the floats for the carnival dotted the tourist section, giving the town a light-hearted and whimsical uniqueness. She assumed that it would be hard to find anything open, and so was thrilled to read an article about the Easter brunch at the Grand Hotel Principe di Piemonte online. Bruno and Bridget had always made a special event of Easter in Italy. She made the reservation several days in advance.

Tammy was already planning to return to Italy to do research for her dual citizenship. She would hunt through church and court documents to support her link to her great grandfather, Michele Paladini. He was from Gorfigliano and her great grandmother, Ottavia Maria Mentessi, was from Roggio. Even though the towns were neighboring, the people of Gorfigliano most likely viewed Ottavia as a foreigner.

On Tammy's last night in Florence they strolled down the hill from Piazzale Michelangelo to I Tarocchi Ristorante Pizzeria. Outside, the evening was still warm. The light was fading in the sky as they watched the candles being lit by the wait staff. Bridget ordered the pear and gorgonzola filled bundles as she had the previous time she and Bruno had come to this hidden gem. She was happy to return to this family-owned trattoria with its typical Tuscan cuisine, lots of locals, and great prices.

The next morning they had a celebratory breakfast of coffee, eggs, and the first Colomba any of them had tried. This was an Easter sweet bread, a widely sold variation on the Christmas favorite, panettone.

Bridget's eyes teared up as Tammy prepared to say good-bye. She was ready to continue her adventure in Italy, and Bridget was counting the days until she would be back in Oregon. The preciousness of this time with Tammy would crown her memories of this trip. They helped Tammy pack even more into her backpack (now the size of a small refrigerator) and take a cab to the train station.

Bruno and Bridget woke up early enough on Easter morning to squeeze in coffee and a big slice of Colomba before walking the mile to the train station. The ride to Viareggio, on the coast west of Florence, took about an hour. The coach wasn't crowded. Bridget wore her ugly walking shoes and carried her sandals. She was dressed in her best outfit, white and black vertical striped calf-length culottes and a black linen jacket. Bruno wore his black blazer and a tie. They looked like sophisticated travelers. When they arrived they had a two-mile walk from the station through the town to the seaside.

Bridget was surprised to see how many people were strolling by the shops featuring beach clothing, plastic beach toys, and sunscreen. Even more of a revelation was the number of informal places to eat that were open. They served seafood platters. Bridget would have been more than happy to call it a fine celebration at any one of these tiny beachfront bistros. Sun worshipers could pay for a brightly colored chair and cabana. Some featured a row of changing closets. It was almost warm enough to consider this.

They walked to the end of the commercial strip to the hotel, where Bridget was anticipating a memorable meal. As they approached the one-story facility on the beach they read the sign that said "Sorry, Closed Until Labor Day."

Bridget's heart sank and her stomach growled. They talked to some other tourists and realized that their destination (with the same name) was the hotel across the street. This thrilled her and she promptly asked Bruno to help steady her as the slipped out of her big black shoes into her sandals.

The Grand Hotel Principe di Piemonte was an Arte Nouveau monument to hospitality. Bruno and Bridget always felt a bit sheepish entering an environment out of their usual range of practicality. They checked in at the front desk. Tables were arrayed in the glassed-in sun porch stretching the length building. By the time they were seated, five formally dressed employees had welcomed them.

Moments later their waiter, who seemed dressed for a ball, poured them prosecco and served them smoked goose breast, soft goat cheese, and brioche.

Next, with a red wine, came a flan of peas, pecorino cheese and crispy pork cheek. Bruno was sure to recreate it back at home. This was the third time they had been served a variation of this sformato type dish on this trip. They were already full, but next came cannelloni filled with a mix of buffalo cheeses and fresh tomato sauce with basil, followed by lamb in Taggiasca olive crust, truffle sauce, potatoes and braised endive with bacon. Their wine glasses were refilled multiple times.

The dessert was cream of pine nuts, honey, and red berry sauce, Italian Easter Colomba and espresso.

The dining room was full. Some tables had family groups with small children in summer shorts and tousled hair. Other families were more formal, with the most senior members sitting in the seats of honor. The dining room sparkled with sunlight and chatter. Bridget and Bruno had fallen on a sweet spot of Easter.

Afterwards, they took a cab to the train station. Strolling the mile back to their apartment gave them almost enough time to digest the unforgettable brunch!

They had one day to pack and pull things together before they would take the train to Rome and fly home. Bridget felt at peace, ready to tuck away another Italian rhapsody.

THE END

Acknowledgments

I would like to thank Cecelia Hagen for her inspiration, poet's touch in editing, and vision. For seventeen years she has led our writing group, the MEADOWLARKS, as we have met and developed our stories: Jo Bogue-Hoffman, Patty Jacobs, Sally Smith, Heidi Sachet, Geraldine Moreno, and Fred Lorish.

Carole Klinich Allen, a lover of Italy and Croatia, generously offered to edit the book. I thank her for her work and big heart.

My sweetheart, John Rose, also offered to edit. He has been my anchor and my compass, and his hand in this tale helped make it all possible as we wandered together in our travels.

Luminare Press once again turned my stories into a beautiful book under the leadership of Patricia Marshall, who has encouraged me. She is a whiz in this book business.